INVESTORS in PEOPLE Explained

SECOND EDITION

Peter Taylor & Bob Thackwray

KOGAN PAGE

First published in 1995
Second edition published in 1996

Apart from any fair dealing for the purposes of research or private study, or
criticism or review, as permitted under the Copyright, Designs and Patents Act,
1988, this publication may only be reproduced, stored or transmitted, in any form
or by any means, with the prior permission in writing of the publishers, or in the
case of reprographic reproduction in accordance with the terms of licences issued
by the Copyright Licensing Agency. Enquiries concerning reproduction outside
those terms should be sent to the publishers at the undermentioned address:

Kogan Page Limited
120 Pentonville Road
London N1 9JN

© Peter Taylor and Bob Thackwray 1995, 1996

The Investors in People Standard is protected by intellectual property rights under
national and international law. The Standard may not be reproduced in whole
or part without prior written consent of Investors in People UK. The Investors in
People mark and logo are protected by trade mark law and may not be used save
in accordance with detailed guidelines issued by Investors in People UK.

For further information regarding the Investors in People, please contact your
local Training and Enterprise Council (TEC) in England and Wales, Local
Enterprise Company (LEC) in Scotland or the Training and Employment Agency
in Northern Ireland. Alternatively write to Investors in People UK, 7–10 Chandos
Street, London W1M 9DE.

British Library Cataloguing in Publication Data

A CIP record for this book is available from the British Library.

ISBN 0 7494 2083 9

Typeset by JS Typesetting, Wellingborough, Northants.
Printed and bound in Great Britain by Biddles Ltd, Guildford and Kings Lynn.

Contents WITHDRAWN

Acknowledgements

The authors gratefully acknowledge the contributions made by a large number of organisations and individuals, especially: Julie Bonner, Monarch Aircraft Engineering; Dawn Clarke, West London Training and Enterprise Council; Robert Dale, Bedfordshire Training and Enterprise Council; Bill Donnelly, National Assessor, Investors in People UK. Terry Evans, Ramada Hotel Heathrow; Steve Franklin, Toyota Motor Manufacturing (UK) Ltd; Heather Hamblin, Open University; Martin Hamilton, Uxbridge Magistrates' Court; Brian Hillier, Manager, Assessment Network Ltd; Bryan Jackson, Toyota Motor Manufacturing (UK) Ltd; Paul Keen, Employment Department, Government Office for North West, (Ex-Acting Chief Executive – Investors in People UK; Tony Lines, Vauxhall Motors; Tony Miller, Frizzell Financial Services Group; John Millward, Uxbridge Magistrates Court; Mike Peart, Mike Peart Associates (MPA) (formerly Employment Department); Ian Plummer, Thomas Bolton Ltd; Leslie Rae, Elrae Associates; John Roberts, Whitbread Pub Partnerships; Juliet Ruggiero, University of Luton; Jeff Thompson, Fujitsu Microelectronics Durham Ltd; and Sue Webb, National Assessors, Investors in People; Jonathon Simnett – A Plus Group; Liz Walling – A Plus Group UK.

Foreword

Developing people: the key to commercial success

In a world where materials, technology and even know-how are widely available and easily transportable, the factor which can make the significant difference in achieving success is the way people are led and managed. Successful organisations of the last two decades have been those that have placed the involvement and development of people at the heart of their business strategies.

Today no one is isolated from international competitive pressures and everyone is challenged by the speed of change, technological advances, short product life-cycles and customer expectations. This all points to one thing – the company with the most skilled, flexible and committed workforce has a competitive edge.

Investors in People is the National Standard for effective investment in people. Developed in 1990, in collaboration with leading UK businesses, it encourages excellence in the field of human resource development. Its aim is to create a culture of continuous self-assessment within organisations, helping to improve business performance by a planned approach to setting and communicating business objectives, and developing people to meet those objectives. The result is that what people can do, and are motivated to do, matches what the organisation needs them to do. The real difference for Investors in People comes from the fact that skilled and motivated people work harder and better, and as a result productivity improves.

Competitive edge

Working towards the Standard means that companies have to review what they are doing against a best-practice benchmark. They then develop an action plan, which is a structured way to improve the effectiveness of training and development activities, so that they help the achievement of business goals. The process is one which leads to improved performance and a competitive edge which secures future prosperity.

Investors in People is much more than training – it is an integration of the human resource strategy with the overall business objectives. It involves a cyclical process based on four key principles which are commitment to develop employees to achieve business goals, reviewing training and development needs, taking action to meet those needs and evaluating the outcome.

Investing in People requires the commitment of everyone in the company, from senior managers to the most junior members of staff. Achieving the standard usually takes between six and eighteen months. However, the principal of developing people to achieve better business effectiveness needs to be ongoing throughout the life of the company. Achieving the Standard is the starting point, and even after recognition experience shows that companies continue to improve.

The journey towards becoming recognised as an Investor in People begins in earnest when a formal written commitment to achieving the Standard is made to a Training and Enterprise Council (TEC), Local Enterprise Company (LEC), or, in Northern Ireland, the Training and Employment Agency. Investors in People UK works in partnership with these organisations, to increase the rate of commitment to and achievement of the Standard.

Guidance and support is provided by the local TEC, LEC or Training and Employment Agency. The services offered may include advisory visits, support materials, networking and seminar workshop events. The help and services are all free – the only direct cost is that of the assessment.

Investors in People status brings public recognition for real achievements measured against a rigorous national Standard. It may provide a reason for customers to choose specific goods and services, and it can help attract the best quality job applicants.

Sir Garry Johnson, Chairman, TEC National Council
Mary Chapman, Chief Executive, Investors in People UK

Introduction

'*Investment in equipment depreciates whilst investment in people appreciates.*' This quote, from Sir Brian Wolfson, captures the theme of this book. Increasingly, organisations are recognising that their most important asset is people. Not to take every possible measure to ensure that all employees contribute fully is bad business. Far too high a percentage of companies that run into difficulties or actually cease to exist cite lack of investment in training as a major contributory factor.

The Investors in People Standard is a mechanism that can provide a framework to support organisations in working out for themselves exactly what is needed, how to go about making it happen and how to evaluate the effectiveness of what has been done. This is not an excessively complicated process: all it requires is commitment and a certain degree of courage. Commitment because the process once started should be continuous: evaluation is not the last thing you do, it occurs throughout every stage of organisational development. After all, what is evaluation if it is not the turning of hindsight into management information? Courage because the process is one of empowerment and enabling, bringing personal and professional development to its rightful place at the heart of strategic planning.

Over the past few years it has become increasingly obvious that the skills and knowledge of people are vital to business success. Employers may well have similar levels of access to the same equipment and materials and yet some organisations are evidently much more successful than others. One of the main reasons for this is that they invest more in their people and like any good investment it pays off. It is often this improvement in the quality of the contribution of all employees that makes the difference between success and failure.

Investors in People is increasingly becoming accepted as the major Standard concerned with helping organisations to address these issues. By 24 March 1996, 3514 organisations had been recognised as an Investor in People – meeting the National Standard for effective investment in people. By the same date another 18,367 organisations had made the commitment to become an Investor in People, involving a total of 5,228,000 people or 24 per cent of the workforce.

This book is designed to be of use and interest to a wide variety of organisations and individuals, and to students and trainers alike, giving a picture of the route to and through the process and incorporating the reflections of various types and sizes of organisations. It seeks to strip away the jargon and to provide the reader with a straightforward and informed account of the origin, development and impact of the Investors in People initiative.

If you or your organisation want to know more about the Standard, or if you are at any stage in the process ranging from thinking about it to heading for re-recognition, this book can provide some answers and, indeed, pose a few more questions!

The book has been designed in three parts. Part One looks at the nature of Investors in People; Part Two describes the experiences of organisations of the various stages in the process; Part Three looks at the way forward. Intended as a working document, this book can be read from beginning to end or particular sections can be dipped into. All sections and chapters can therefore be read independently of the rest: they are 'stand alone' accounts of a particular element of the process.

Part One: The Process

Chapter 1 covers the Origins and Development of Investors in People – who was involved, its launch, what it set out to achieve and why.

In Chapter 2 we answer the question What is Investors in People?

We will explain how the concept fits with managing change, supporting business development; how it links to Total Quality and the concept of continuous improvement. Of particular importance here is the point that it should not be seen as an additional task but that it can be integrated into business processes. For those organisations, trainers and students who would like to see how Investors in People links to the concept of a 'learning organisation', Chapter 11 examines this in some detail.

In Chapter 3, Why Bother? we outline in general terms what organisations who have already been recognised as Investors in People say they have gained from the process. As well as covering the 'added value' from the corporate point of view it looks at what is in it for individuals.

Chapter 4 should be of interest to all. It explains how Investors in People actually works. It covers how to get started on 'The Journey' (which many say is more important than the destination) by addressing such key questions as:

- Where am I now?
- What about the things I am already doing or am planning to do?
- How to involve the people?
- What is needed to be done?
- Who does it?
- How long will it take?
- What will it cost?

The chapter also tries to dispel some of the myths that have grown up about Investors in People such as worries about bureaucracy and whether it is just a flavour of the month initiative.

Chapter 5 examines The Role of the Line Manager. A key player in the process, the involvement of the line manager, and the nature of that involvement, is of crucial importance to the success of the venture.

Chapter 6 sets the Organisation and the Role of the Assessor in context. It looks at what 'evidence' is and how best to prepare for assessment. It will also give some tips on building up the portfolio of evidence. Using their experience of the assessment process, the authors will describe what the process entails and what an assessor's role is, how people are chosen for interview and some of the questions that may be asked.

Chapter 7 follows on from assessment through the Recognition Process and describes the 'Recognition Panel' and how it works. It will also look at what recognition means and how long it remains in force.

Chapter 8, the Indicators Explained, takes on the task of looking at what lies behind the 23 revised indicators and their structure and purpose.

Finally in this section, Chapter 9 looks at particular challenges facing Large and Multi-sited Organisations.

Part Two: The Experiences

What was it like for some of those organisations who have already become Investors in People or are on the journey? This part of the book includes a number of case-studies that reveal the highs and lows of the 'journey' and what they gained from the experience. The organisations selected were chosen for reasons of size, type and nature of activity and the variety of experience they collectively offered.

The organisations included as case-studies are: Bedfordshire Training and Enterprise Council; Thomas Bolton Ltd; Frizzell Financial Services Group; Fujitsu Microelectronics Durham Ltd; Monarch Aircraft Engineering; The Open University and the University of Luton; Ramada Hotel Heathrow; Toyota Motor Manufacturing (UK) Ltd; Uxbridge Magistrates' Court; Vauxhall Motors; and Whitbread Pub Partnerships and the A Plus Group.

Part Three: Next Steps

To plateau or not to plateau? Things have a habit of going a little cold after an important event such as achieving recognition. Chapter 10, Maintaining and Retaining Recognition, looks at this and makes some recommendations set in the context of a number of changes within the Investors in People process itself. In addition current issues concerning the reassessment process are explored.

In this final part of the book Chapter 11 takes the process to the next stage. In Learning to be a Learning Organisation, we pull together some of the key issues and set the Investors process in the context of the learning organisation.

Chapter 12 gives some information about Sources of Help for those organisations who would like to pursue Investors in People further. It explains the roles of the various sources of help and information including consultants and the contributions they can be expected to make and includes the role of consultants in the process.

Finally, there are four appendices. The first one gives the full National Standard and the 23 revised indicators. The second is Investors in People: Manager's Survey. The third is an Investors in People Employees' Survey, and the fourth is the Investors in People UK Sample Size Guidelines.

CHAPTER 1

Origins and Development

This chapter explores how Investors in People evolved in the seven years since its beginnings in 1989. It also examines the roles of people and organisations involved in the various stages of its development. This chapter will be of particular interest and value to students, teachers and trainers and to all those with a general interest in the background and development of Investors in People. We will seek to answer the often-asked questions, 'How was it developed?' and 'Where did it come from?' by looking at how the Investors in People initiative developed and at the people and organisations involved.

The beginning

The Investors in People process arose out of repeated reports which demonstrated that, compared to our competitors, Britain's existing workforce held fewer qualifications. One report, *Training in Britain 1987*, published by the Training Agency of the Department of Employment, drew attention to the fact that although £18 billion per annum was spent on training, employers in Great Britain did not spend as much as their competitors and the skills gap was widening. Clearly, something needed to be done.

The stakeholders

The key players in the development of Investors in People were:

- the National Training Task Force;
- the CBI; and
- the Department of Employment.

The National Training Task Force (NTTF)

The NTTF was set up by the Department of Employment as a result of the 1988 Government White Paper 'Employment for the 1990s'. As well as setting the NTTF the task of establishing a network of Training and Enterprise Councils it also gave them the remit to 'promote to employers the necessity of their investing in the skills of the working population'. The then Chairman of the NTTF, Sir Brian Wolfson, Chairman of Wembley plc, set up a subgroup to examine how this might be achieved.

The subgroup included members of the NTTF, some of the chairmen of the first TECs, and representatives from other interested parties such as the TUC, CBI, and the Association of British Chambers of Commerce, Wales and Scotland.

The CBI

While this activity was taking place the CBI had also established a task force, led by Sir Bryan Nicholson, to look at similar issues. Their report, *Towards a Skills Revolution*, came up with the concept of an 'Investor in Training', for which it included ten principles.

We present those principles (Figure 1.1) as indicative of the thinking behind the development of Investors in People and because a considerable degree of consistency is evident as the process matures.

These principles and the conclusions reached by the CBI Task Force were very similar to those reached by the NTTF. Compare the above principles with the Investors in People Standard and it can be seen just how influential they were in subsequent developments.

The report also set a number of targets. One of the most significant was that 'by 1995 at least half of all medium sized and larger companies should qualify as "Investors in Training" as assessed by the relevant Training and Enterprise Council'. This target would later be amended, replacing 'Investors in Training' with

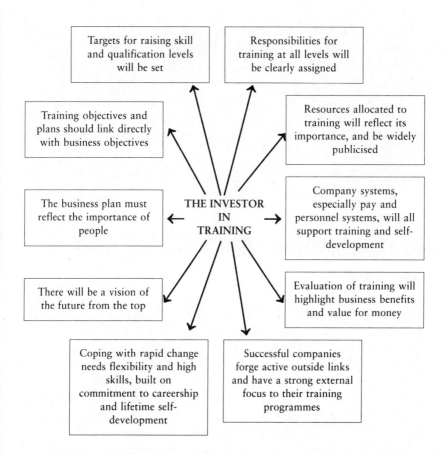

Figure 1.1 *The ten principles of an Investor in Training*

'Investors in People', after some considerable amount of research on naming the initiative had been undertaken.

The paper was launched at the CBI Conference in Harrogate in November 1989. At the conference Norman Fowler, then Secretary of State for Employment, responded to the CBI paper by proposing that the NTTF work with the CBI and with other business and training organisations, including TECs, to develop an 'action programme'.

The Department of Employment

This subgroup commissioned officials from the Department of Employment to consider what employers would have to do to invest in their people. The Department had developed a number of initiatives throughout the 1980s and undoubtedly the research that preceded those initiatives and their subsequent evaluation influenced the ideas that were produced. Also in late 1989 a small team was established at the Department's Sheffield headquarters to coordinate this activity.

The outcomes were presented to the NTTF and the findings were reported to the Secretary of State.

Action and growth: The emergence of the Standard

Following the conference a working group of practitioners was established who would work to develop the idea of the 'action programme'. The group of practitioners included representatives from a number of government departments, TEC chief executives, CBI, Institute of Personnel Management (IPM), Institute of Training & Development (ITD), Trades Union Congress (TUC), National Council for Vocational Qualifications (NCVQ), industry training organisations and the Association of British Chambers of Commerce. Their remit was to consider and develop proposals and make recommendations to the NTTF subgroup. Over the next 6–9 months the action programme concept was moulded and developed. The idea of a standard based on good practice was mooted.

The criteria chosen for the standard were based on best practice of selected employers. No one employer was used as the model. The Investor in People Standard was drawn up as a result of studying the good practice of a wide range of successful organisations in all sectors of the economy. As already indicated, it was also influenced considerably by the CBI's ten principles for an 'Investor in Training'. Finally, it also took into account lessons learnt from a variety of the Employment Department's initiatives with employers, including the National Training Awards and Business Growth Training.

One overriding principle was that employers should not feel that this initiative involved government officials and ministers telling them how to run their business. It was not and should not be presented as a top-down initiative. Whatever was developed had to allow businesses to meet the criteria in a way that offered clearly perceived and measurable benefits to their individual business.

An early outline of the criteria was drawn up and Coopers & Lybrand were commissioned to test out the validity of both the concept and content with a sample of 20 employers carefully chosen by the Department and the consultants to be 'representative', ie by size, sector, location etc. The report from this research would also provide case-study material of what employers actually did in practice. Research outcomes clearly indicated the need for an assessment framework. This led to Price Waterhouse being commissioned to develop such a framework.

From July 1990 some of the early TECs and the then residual Area Offices of the Training Agency and the Office for Scotland were invited to pilot the concept with employers in their areas. These pilots were the first stage in selling the potential benefits of the initiative to the people who would eventually have to run with it. The pilots met with mixed levels of success but in general confirmed significant interest levels among employers.

Where did the name Investors in People come from?

While the pilots were progressing, market research was being undertaken to establish the name. The research was carried out by Makrotest (now CEGOS Makrotest) throughout June and July 1990. A number of key words and slogans were brainstormed and tested out with a sample of 500 business people and associated agencies, the testing involving a mixture of telephone research and group discussion, and the outcome was presented to the NTTF Sub-Group together with a logo that had been designed. Their decision resulted in the current logo and the name 'Investors in People'.

The launch

The name was announced and the national Standard launched by Michael Howard, Secretary of State for Employment, at the CBI Conference in Glasgow in November 1990.

Price Waterhouse, meanwhile, were developing the assessment framework. This work, together with the continuation of the pilots and an invitation to TEC staff to identify companies which they felt to be close to meeting the criteria, culminated in around 40 companies being assessed during the summer of 1991. Of these, 28 met the 'standard' and were subsequently recognised at a media event held in London on 16 October 1991. In addition to recognising the first Investors in People the event also provided a summary of progress to date and listed those companies which had made a commitment to work towards the Standard.

For these first assessments the process was overseen by KPMG Peat Marwick who reported that the assessment framework had proven robust. Adjustments were made to the wording of some of the performance indicators as a result of this exercise, but these were in the main quite minor. Some of the early concerns voiced by employers in particular were about potential bureaucracy and the quality of the assessors. In particular, how could it be ensured that the 'national Standard' would be applied nationally?

Throughout the next 18 months quality assurance measures were established to address these issues. The lessons learnt from the first assessments were disseminated to all those who had been involved and thereafter to those who were to be drawn in later.

The twin terrors of bureaucracy and interference still surface today. In the following chapters we will demonstrate that such worries are groundless if the organisation has, or wishes to have, a culture that sees the benefits of continuous professional development for all its employees.

The demise of the NTTF

When the NTTF had been established it was given four years to complete its task (as described earlier in this chapter) and at the end of 1992 it therefore ceased to exist. The NTTF subgroup set up by Sir Brian Wolfson had developed a number of roles during the previous 15 months which would create a vacuum if it too was wound up so it was agreed that this group under the chairmanship of Sir Allen (now Lord) Sheppard, Chairman and Chief Executive Officer of Grand Metropolitan plc, would continue to carry out their role. This role had been widened to cover all aspects of Employer Investment (in their workforce). The enhanced role included:

- overseeing the further development of the initiative;
- recognition of those TECs that had been assessed by National Assessors as having met the criteria;
- recognition of some large and multi-sited organisations who had chosen to go as a whole.

In the spring of 1993 a successor body to the NTTF was announced, named the National Advisory Committee for Education and Training Targets (NACETT) and given the remit of encouraging organisations to work towards the National Education and Training Targets.

The establishment of Investors in People UK

The subgroup continued to operate until the end of June 1993. On 1 July a new body, Investors in People UK, was established and chaired by Sir Brian Wolfson. The membership of this body was appointed by the Secretary of State following consultation with the TEC movement.

It was announced that this body would have an executive arm, a private company limited by guarantee, which would take over some of the work that had previously been undertaken by officials in the Department of Employment. A Chief Executive Officer, Mary Chapman, formerly Director of Personnel Operations and Management Development with the L'Oréal Group in the UK, took up the post on 1 December 1993.

The role of Investors in People UK is to:

1. be 'protector' of the national Standard;
2. market and promote Investors in People nationally;
3. provide a national assessment and quality assurance service.

The first stages in taking this role forward were marketing strategies:

1. January 1994 launching the company:
2. Conference for Chief Executives of major companies held in May 1994:
3. 'Investors in People Weeks' during October 1994 and October 1995.

They have introduced licences for training providers to train assessors. Since its early days Investors in People has attracted a great deal of interest from abroad, notably from Australia, where it is being piloted. Investors in People UK are exploring the possibility of licensing/franchising the concept overseas.

Subsequent chapters in this book will outline the process of becoming an Investor in People and the involvement of the TECs. Arrangements in Scotland and Northern Ireland are slightly different, the more significant differences are outlined opposite.

Investors in Scotland

Scotland has Local Enterprise Companies (LECs) instead of TECs. Although LECs carry out the same basic functions as TECs they also have an enhanced role as they also carry out the functions of either Scottish Enterprise or Highlands and Islands Enterprise. The decision was taken early in the development of Investors in People to set up a separate company, Investors in People Scotland Ltd, which would carry out assessments on behalf of the LECs. All the work prior to assessment is carried out by the LECs.

This model will be examined further in Chapters 6 and 7.

Investors in Northern Ireland

Northern Ireland has neither TECs nor LECs. Their role is carried out by the government Training and Employment Agency. The Agency's involvement with Investors in People began in early 1993, with their first recognitions of companies as Investors in People in October of that year. The Agency carries out the same role as TECs in England and Wales and will be referred to throughout the following chapters.

The review of the Standard

It was always intended that the national Standard should be reviewed to ensure that it remained at the leading edge of human resource development. The project to review the Standard and make recommendations on its future development took place during 1995. The objectives of the review were:

- to ensure the continued relevance and credibility of Investors in People as a framework for organisation improvement and as a benchmark of good practice;

- to anticipate future trends in people management and organisation development;
- to position the Standard accordingly in the wider context of quality management initiatives, standards and awards.

Following consultation and debate, the revisions were agreed early in 1996 and the revised indicators are scheduled to come out during the summer. All organisations being assessed after 31 January 1997 will be assessed against the revised indicators.

The actual changes comprise some rewording of individual indicators to provide greater clarity and therfore more consistent interpretation; some indicators have been relocated to improve the link between indicators; the evaluation indicators have been reordered and overlapping indicators have been combined. The standard itself has not changed nor is it 'more difficult to achieve'.

Summary

We have described how Investors in People was created by the work of the CBI, the National Training Task Force and the Department of Employment. The chapter has explored how the process and materials were developed and piloted prior to the formal recognition of the first Investors in People in 1991 and has charted the establishment of the new national body, Investors in People UK.

CHAPTER 2

What is Investors in People?

This chapter is essential reading. It explains what Investors in People is and how it can support business development, and shows that it should not be viewed as additional work but an integral part of what ought to be everyday business activity. This is examined in context with other contemporary initiatives such as Total Quality and ISO 9000/BS5750. The chapter also shows how Investors in People can effectively be used in support of the management of change.

The concept

The central focus of Investors in People is the national Standard for Effective Investment in People. This is now more commonly known as the Investors in People Standard (see Figure 2.1).

The concept is deceptively simple. Employing organisations are encouraged to meet the Standard. If they do, they will be recognised as an Investor in People; if they don't, they will be encouraged to take the required action to meet it.

As indicated in Chapter 1 the Standard is based on good practice and therefore meeting it makes good business sense. We have yet to find anyone who disagrees with the principles underpinning the Standard. This does not, of course, mean that actually going for recognition as an Investor in People is universally regarded as a good thing. On the contrary, some organisations express strong views as to why they feel it is inappropriate for them.

Training is an investment, not a cost

It is increasingly accepted that the single most important factor differentiating one company from another is the skills, knowledge and expertise of its people. Most have access to similar ranges of equipment, technology and other facilities. Therefore it is how well these are used that makes the difference. The service sector especially relies considerably on the skills and attitudes of people to demonstrate commitment to the efficient delivery of a quality service.

That notwithstanding, research continually demonstrates that large numbers of organisations do not consider training and development of people as an investment. They see it as a cost. It is therefore not planned strategically nor is it clearly linked to business objectives. It is not equally available to all employees. It is rarely evaluated at the point of delivery, let alone later in terms of its impact on effectiveness of working practices.

If this is the case then the question arises 'how much is wasted?' Can something be done to ensure that training and development budgets are spent more effectively?

What is new about Investors in People?

Very little! The Investors in People Standard is based on standards of good practice that a wide range of organisations have been employing to greater or lesser degrees for some time, as mentioned in Chapter 1. What is new, therefore, is that good practice, having been taken from this range of organisations, has been packaged

Principle One: Commitment
An Investor in People makes a commitment from the top to develop all employees to achieve its business objectives.

Principle Two: Planning
An Investor in People regularly reviews the needs and plans the training and development of all employees.

Principle Three: Action
An Investor in People takes action to train and develop individuals on recruitment and throughout their employment.

Principle Four: Evaluation
An Investor in People evaluates the investment in training and development to assess achievement and improve future effectiveness.

Figure 2.1 *Investors in People Standard*

together in a coherent way. It is consequently in a position to offer organisations a framework which has potential to be used strategically to tackle a range of business issues and their linked training and development activities. This framework is examined in the following chapters. It follows therefore that training and development can and should become integrated into the culture of the organisation.

Another new feature is the formal recognition. This can be used by an organisation to show the outside world what has been achieved. Investors in People status increasingly results (albeit more slowly than the targets initially set for it) in well trained and better motivated workforces.

Most organisations that have started work on becoming an Investor in People see the 'journey' as far more important than the actual destination. This, of course, is entirely within the spirit that created Investors in People in the first place. Although there are legitimate benefits to be gained from being recognised as an Investor in People, the real gain is in going through the process. There are benefits for all, but it is clear that those organisations furthest away from meeting the Standard will have the most to gain.

Is it just another training initiative?

Those who worked on its creation and the majority of recognised organisations would say definitely not. Although organisations that have 'travelled the Investors in People journey' may have started by thinking it was only about training, they all confirm that it has turned out to be much more. A large number have said it has had a major impact on the way their organisation carries out its business. (See the case-studies; Chapter three; and later in this chapter.)

What are the main features of an Investor in People?

An organisation that is an Investor in People will:

- plan ahead and have clear measurable objectives that are continually monitored and updated;
- be clear what skills and knowledge are needed to achieve its goals and targets and deliver the plan;
- have identified what skills and knowledge the people already have;
- plan and take action to fill any gaps between the skills and knowledge already held and those needed;
- will look back after the action has been taken to see what impact it has had on the business, whether the action was effective in filling the gap, and if it was not, take further action.

All such action will be taken in the context of the needs and direction of the business. As business needs and directions constantly change and develop, new gaps will be created and further action taken. As there is also a need for organisations to strive for continuous improvement in order to maintain performance, rather like painting the Forth Road Bridge, the task never ends. Achieving Investors in People status therefore is merely a milestone on the journey. Retaining the status is the next milestone.

The 'framework' or 'model'

It can be difficult to see how the Standard as illustrated in Figure 2.1 can be described as a 'framework' or 'model' of good practice.

Nor is it easy to assess an organisation against the Standard in that form. The Standard has therefore been broken down into 23 'indicators' against which an organisation can be assessed. These indicators are reproduced at Appendix 1, and Chapter 8 explores the meaning and function of each one and how they link together. It is, therefore, the indicators that become the 'framework' that can then be used in support of organisations in a variety of situations, as illustrated below.

Developing the business and business development

The above title may appear to suggest that this section may only be relevant to private sector organisations. As is now well documented, there is increasing pressure on public and voluntary sector organisations to be more accountable, more efficient and, in some cases, to generate income. Business development may therefore be of particular relevance to them.

From the first organisations to be recognised has emerged evidence that Investors in People has contributed significantly to business performance.

- *Increased sales*, eg Land Rover up 33 per cent 1991–93; Deritend Precision Castings up 74 per cent 1990–93; Bettys and Taylors of Harrogate up 33 per cent 1990–93.
- *Cost improvement*, eg Brooke Bond Foods, Worksop cost per tonne decreased by 22 per cent 1992–93; The Cumberland Hotel, northwest London, 35 per cent cost savings 1991–93.
- *Profitability*, eg Woolwich Building Society pre-tax profits rose by 45 per cent 1992–93; De Vere Hotels gross profit increased by 15.2 per cent 1992–93.

The management of change and the changing of management

All organisations are facing change of some description. Typical corporate changes currently include delayering or flattening structures, multi-skilling or flexible working practices and the introduction or improvement of quality approaches. Change is not now seen as undesirable, of course. As innovation and improvement oriented management philosophies and methodologies bite ever deeper into the reality of everyday working life, so managed and directed change becomes essential to organisational competitiveness, development and growth. Certainly, the ability to handle change more quickly and more effectively than competitors is a key issue in maintaining business performance.

For some, when facing change, knowing where to start can be the most difficult part. Within the Investors in People Standard there are a number of frameworks or models that can be used to facilitate this process. For example, the standard offers a framework by which aims and objectives can be clarified, and become more focused and planned. It also offers models for implementing, monitoring and reviewing progress.

The changes mentioned above invariably have a major impact on the role of line managers. Delayering leads to having fewer managers; having flexible and/or multi-skilled teams leads to changes in the way staff are managed. Line managers are clearly key players in helping their organisation achieve Investors in People status (for a more in-depth examination of the part they can play see Chapter 5, The Role of the Line Manager).

Investors in People and quality

Whether operating in the manufacturing or the service sector, quality of product or service is a critical factor and necessarily sets an organisation apart from its competitors. There are so many different approaches to quality improvement and many books that concentrate on these approaches that this section merely aims to highlight linkages.

Currently, the most popular approach is to introduce quality systems, usually opting for ISO 9000 (formerly BS5750). Quality systems generally underpin the approach to quality. They will involve a significant investment and rely on people to adhere to the systems. Training is therefore the significant component when introducing these systems, so that they are not only adhered to but also understood. Many organisations feel that if they are introducing quality systems they 'have enough on their plates without introducing Investors in People as well'. If the Investors in People Standard is correctly used as the framework for the introduction of the systems it should not create extra work: it should merely ensure that the training associated with it follows good practice and is effective.

Investors in People is not merely about training. A by-product of the simultaneous introduction of Investors in People and quality systems will be that other changes, often cultural, will take place, leading organisations to a further stage in quality improvement often called Total Quality. A number of organisations and writers on management theory and practice would argue that quality systems plus Investors in People is very close to the concept of 'Total Quality'. Careful examination of the Standard reveals that it is very close to the favoured 'plan–do–check' concept favoured by some Total Quality gurus.

Another approach to quality improvement, especially in the service sector, is to have Customer Service Statements; or in the public sector to link it to the Citizen's Charter. Implementing these approaches involves training and development but most of all it should mean a change of culture leading to increased commitment from staff to delivering a quality service and meeting increasingly demanding customer expectations. Using the Investors in People framework can help achieve this.

Organisational development

The changes mentioned above usually lead to the formation of new teams and sometimes to the formation of teams for the first time! Some will be permanent whereas others will have been brought together to work cross-functionally. Whatever the situation, the members of new teams need to learn to work together and frequently the first steps are to have a number of teambuilding events. Again, the Investors in People Standard can offer a framework for teambuilding. Clarity of purpose is the starting-point for any teambuilding activity and the first part of the Standard can be used as a model, the subsequent parts to plan, implement, control and evaluate the process.

Investors in People and redundancy

A number of organisations have been recognised as Investors in People while at the same time making people redundant. There are three key considerations in this situation. First, the people who are not being made redundant will probably face different roles when the others have left. Secondly, they will have training and development needs. Thirdly, those who are leaving may need help to secure other jobs. Therefore the approach of the employer towards providing back-up can have an effect on those made redundant, on their customers and also on those staying on, who may feel reassured that if further redundancies are necessary they too will be helped. Nevertheless, the point must be made that Investors in People is not an automatic guarantee of job satisfaction and continuity and it should not be presented as such.

Clearly when introducing the concept of Investors in People in these situations sensitive handling is essential, with organisational and individual benefits being the main focus.

Investors in People and the concept of a learning organisation

The concept of a learning organisation developed out of the self-development movement which began in the 1970s. This movement stressed the need for individuals to take responsibility for addressing their own training and career development needs. In order to enable this to happen organisations need to create the right environment. However there are many definitions of what actually constitutes a 'learning organisation'.

During the last few years interest and debate around the concept has increased. Clearly the issues that have been outlined in this chapter are pertinent to the debate but perhaps readers may want to explore them. They are therefore outlined in detail in Chapter 11, Learning to be a Learning Organisation.

What's in it for individuals?

Most of what has been written in this chapter has focused on the needs of organisations. The process is designed to place training and development needs at the centre of the corporate agenda by linking them to the business planning process. Clearly for most organisations training demands that lie well outside these corporate parameters cannot always be met. Investors in People is not a mandate to provide any or all training requested. That notwithstanding, clear evidence does now exist that shows that pay in recognised organisations has increased significantly greater than that of organisations generally. (See Chapter 3, Why Bother?)

Investors in People and Continuous Professional Development (CPD)

For those individuals who are members of professional institutions the concept of continuous professional development (CPD) will be familiar. Most, if not all, institutions now demand that to maintain their membership, members must provide evidence of CPD.

This concept sits readily within Investors in People. In this instance the framework can be applied to an individual: plan, take action and evaluate.

As well as satisfying individual requirements the achievement of CPD will also provide evidence for the organisation.

Investors in People and succession planning

It has sometimes been argued that succession planning and development beyond the needs of the immediate job are not catered for in the Investors in People Standard. This is not true. The first parts of the Standard are a framework for strategic planning for both the business and the people to deliver the plans. This must include succession planning and the resultant development needs of the people.

Summary

This chapter has attempted to clarify and explain how Investors in People is not merely about training; that it is not something that is bolted on to other initiatives associated with business development; that it should be an integral part of everyday business activity.

The links to a variety of contemporary business issues have been explored as have the ways in which the Investors in People Standard can be used as a framework or model to manage the various issues associated with change that face modern businesses.

CHAPTER 3

Why Bother?

We now examine the question of why bother, for those readers who are still not convinced that Investors in People has anything to offer them.

'You can't afford not to' is a popular response, and versions of it are used by promoters of Investors in People all over the UK. Is it true? What are the perceived benefits of the process? Does it confer a range of advantages on the company or institution as is claimed? What are the views of those who have gone through the process, those who are going through the process and those who do not currently want to? What are the concerns?

The latest statistics

At the time of writing, nearly five years after the initiative was launched in October 1991, some 3,514 (1,960 in May 1995) companies, organisations and autonomous units within organisations have achieved the standard and 18,367 (16,383 in May 1995) were committed (source: Investors in People UK). The first batch of companies to achieve recognition have gone through the process of re-recognition and most have been re-recognised.

An IRS survey of employers' experience published in March 1994 demonstrated that after a 'painfully slow start' participation was increasing. At that time only 677 were recognised but 5,630 were committed. Interestingly, these figures were to jump considerably even by the end of that month (to 739 recognitions and over 6,300 commitments). Clearly interest was on the up – as our later figures demonstrate. But whose interest? The IRS survey noted that about two-thirds of organisations achieving recognition were small companies (ie employed less than 200 people). Another significant feature coming out of the survey was that over a quarter were organisations whose business was education and training. This is hardly surprising: it is obvious that a national standard for training and development would be much sought after by such organisations, and that they would often be in a position to learn of and react to the Investor in People initiative more quickly than most other organisations.

The expectation would be, however, that this trend would at the very least flatten out. In 1996 this does appear to be the case although the expansion of interest in further and higher education is remarkable with, for example, over 70 universities committed either as a whole or with an autonomous unit, and five whole higher education institutions recognised, the first of which, the University of Luton, is featured as a case-study later in this book.

During the first three years the ratio of recognised organisations employing under 200 to those employing over 200 was constant at 2:1. As 96 per cent of employers in Great Britain employ fewer than 20 people, this statistic shows that the ratio of large companies is good. However, concern has been expressed that not enough blue chip companies are coming forward, though it is difficult to be exact about this as large companies are tending to approach Investors in People by piloting in small autonomous units (see Chapter 9). To address this concern, Investors in People UK have established a pilot programme, with the aim of taking 15 multi-nationals to recognition.

People *are* bothering – why?

Evidently, the question why bother is being answered positively by an increasing number and variety of companies and organisations. Reasons for participation vary but several common themes emerge and not all of these are consistent with some of the reasons 'sold' by Training and Enterprise Councils (profit/efficiency etc).

A considerable number of companies and organisations believe their current training and development practice is good and they wish to have this recognised. Given that the assessment process provides a 'snapshot' of how an organisation feels about itself at a particular moment in time, the process affords organisations the opportunity to test this belief out by external benchmarking (see case studies on Toyota UK, Vauxhall Motors and Monarch Aircraft Engineering).

The IRS table (Table 3.1) lists reasons by popularity. Of some surprise is the fact that only 4.8 per cent cited improving the reputation of the company among customers. This relates closely to a major reason for non participation: 'we'll do it when the customers demand it'. This must be an area for Investors in People UK to address. It is interesting to note that ensuring that training activity is focused on business needs came out strongly which is a message the TECs consistently stress.

The actual benefits

An examination of the case-study companies later in this book shows the following benefits:

- it leads to the clarification and communication of business objectives (*Monarch Aircraft Engineering*);
- it leads to a special focus on administration staff who had been overlooked (*Monarch Aircraft Engineering*);
- it increased involvement of managers in driving individual development (*Fujitsu Microelectronics*);

- the Investors framework was useful in bringing together a number of seemingly unrelated activities (*University of Luton*).

Investors in People UK case-studies show that the 60 recognised organisations they surveyed are quoting the following benefits to which Investors in People has contributed:

- increased profitability (*Boots the Chemist, ICL, De Vere Hotels*);
- increased efficiency (*Hydro Polymers, IBS*);
- increased sales and income (*Land Rover, Bettys and Taylors of Harrogate, Lawdon Mardon Plastics*);
- reduced costs (*Brooke Bond Foods – Worksop, IDV UK – Essex*).

A number of organisations referred to Investors in People as stimulating continuous improvement initiatives and others talk of improved management skills. There were also benefits for individuals such as improved opportunities for skill and career development, and access to qualifications.

Individuals also referred to managers managing more effectively which led to increased involvement, support/encouragement and recognition. The overriding message is

improved communication = better informed people
= increased commitment.

So why do some organisations not bother?

Experience has shown that the most common reasons for not proceeding concern the cost of the process and the potential bureaucracy. Many organisations wonder what value it adds, especially if they believe they are doing the right things already. Even organisations who are interested and see potential benefits frequently dither about the final decision. They often say it's the wrong time:

Table 3.1 *Reasons for seeking Investors in People*

Reasons	1	2	3	4
To get recognition for good training practice	73.8	23.5	59.6	8.7
To ensure that training activity relates directly to business needs	71.6	25.9	84.6	39.1
To provide a focus for training and development activities	66.1	4.2	86.5	15.2
To motivate employees	66.1	5.4	71.2	2.2
To audit training and development activity against a national benchmark	62.8	13.3	61.5	2.2
To improve the reputation of the company among customers	56.8	4.8	44.2	2.2
To improve the quality of products/services	42.1	4.2	50.0	4.3
To facilitate change in the organisation	40.4	7.8	59.6	10.9
To raise standards of customer service	39.3	3.6	50.0	6.5
To get publicity for the organisation	33.3	0.6	21.5	2.2
To increase productivity	25.1	0.6	23.1	–
To improve the amount of training in the organisation	23.0	0.6	48.1	4.3
Were persuaded by marketing of IiP by the local TEC/LEC	20.2	1.2	5.8	–
To take advantage of grants/financial assistance offered by TECs/LECs	18.6	1.8	28.8	–
To reduce costs	18.0	–	23.1	–
Because competitors were committed to gaining IiP	5.5	1.2	11.5	2.2
	(183)	(166)	(52)	(46)

1 *Achievers citing (all reasons)*

2 *Achievers citing (main reason)*

3 *Committed citing (all reasons)*

4 *Committed citing (main reason)*

Source: *Investors in People UK*. IRS survey, March 1994.

'we're too busy planning'
'we have too many changes on the go at the moment'
'we are in the middle of introducing ISO 9000 (BS5750/Total Quality)'
'we are in the middle of a redundancy exercise'

Investors in People is often seen as another task rather than a tool or framework to help manage these situations. Many of the recognised organisations introduced Investors in People while dealing with the above situations.

The worry about the consistency of assessment

Many organisations, especially large and multi-sited ones, are concerned that although the focus of Investors in People is a *national* standard, assessment is spread around the whole of the UK and therefore they are worried about assessors interpreting the indicators differently.

Summary

This chapter has examined some of the reasons that have influenced organisations to commit to Investors in People. It has also detailed some of the benefits quoted by organisations that have achieved recognition. It has looked at some of the reasons and concerns that have stopped organisations from making the commitment.

The rest of the book addresses most of these issues to enable readers to make up their own minds.

CHAPTER 4

The Journey

There is a consensus among recognised organisations that suggests that the journey is more important than the destination. In other words, as indicated throughout this book, the process as developed and implemented by the organisation is the most significant element in the success or failure of Investors in People.

This chapter is therefore of particular importance as it explains the stages in the journey and what they involve. It answers such questions as:

- how do I start?
- how long will it take?
- how much will it cost?

It will also address the issue of how bureaucratic the journey need be and the longevity of Investors in People (two other areas of concern). There is, it will be demonstrated, clear potential for organisations to benefit from every stage of the Investors process. It should be remembered at all times that action being taken is to improve the organisation's effectiveness, not to meet the Investors in People Standard for its own sake. The Standard is based on best practice, so action to meet it should lead to improved effectiveness.

However – before reading this chapter – a few words of warning for those readers seeking the ideal approach to meet the Investors in People Standard. They may be disappointed to find that there is no *one* approach. Nevertheless, by reading the following chapters and the case-study experiences in Part Two they should be able to identify appropriate methods that meet the needs of their own organisations. The 'secret' is to interpret the indicators in a way that suits the culture of the organisation.

Where are you now?

The first thing that any organisation needs to do is to find out how it currently compares with the Standard. This is where the 23 indicators, as reproduced in Appendix 1, come into play again as it is against these that the comparison, often called a *diagnosis*, should be made.

Organisations enter the process at different levels of sophistication with regard to training and development. There is also a wide variety of corporate cultures: strong, weak, directed, undirected, positive, negative, to mention but a few extremes. For a large number of organisations the decision to make a commitment involves possibly the most challenging decision in the whole process. It can seem like a step into the dark and may feel threatening. Indicators that at first glance seem clear take on a sometimes disconcerting complexity when applied to your own organisation. They may then seem confusing, giving rise to concern and doubt as to how far away from meeting the Standard the organisation actually is. This then leads to the question of how much time commitment actually entails.

These legitimate concerns can be offset by consideration of the fact that most organisations will have a number of systems and processes in existence that will go some way to meeting a number of the indicators. Occasionally these may be very obvious but sometimes they need to be interpreted in order to satisfy the indicator. Again, the focus is on the enhancement of existing good practice and the introduction of structured systemic improvements. It is not a test. There are a number of sources of help with interpretation and guidance for organisations going through or thinking about going through the process, including Training and Enterprise Councils, a wide variety of independent consultants and trainers and some colleges and universities. (See Chapter 12 for sources of help.)

All organisations will at one time or another be raising some or all of the above questions and concerns. Investors in People provides an opportunity for them to be addressed in a coherent and consistent manner via the diagnostic stage.

Diagnostic methods

There are a number of methods employed in carrying out this stage. It can be tempting to give one or two people the task of examining the indicators and ticking off which they think the organisation meets. These staff are often senior managers and often include the Personnel or Training Manager. This approach may give a broad indication but it depends very heavily on the knowledge and depth of understanding of the realities of the organisation's corporate culture at a range of levels of the managers who take part.

To get a fairly accurate analysis it is essential to involve a cross-section of staff from all levels. This cross-section should be a diagonal slice of the organisation, taking on board the various criteria set out for assessors (as described in Chapter 6). The existence of systems and processes does not always mean they actually work. Employees who are genuinely encouraged to be honest and open in a threat-free environment will give an organisation a realistic assessment.

Given the above criteria, the most successful (and now, therefore, the most often used) approaches incorporate elements of the following :

- carrying out a confidential survey using questionnaires that have been customised to suit each individual organisation; or
- inviting a qualified person, normally from outside the

organisation, to carry out a combination of a survey and interviews.

The questionnaires and/or interview questions should be designed in such a way as to determine which of the 23 indicators are met satisfactorily and which are not. Normally two sets of questionnaires are used, one for managers and one for the remaining employees. Examples of the two types of questionnaire are in Appendices 2 and 3.

The decision about where to draw the line between who should complete the managers' survey and who should complete the employees' surveys is often not easy. Middle and junior managers could in fact complete both as they manage staff and are themselves managed. The normal approach will be to draw the line towards the upper level of middle managers in larger organisations. In smaller organisations the line will probably be drawn below the senior management team. It is really up to each organisation to make this decision in a way that will draw out the most useful information for them from the survey.

The results from the survey often reveal that managers believe they are managing staff effectively. Equally often, their staff disagree.

Analysis of the findings of their survey should then give an indication of how close or how far away the organisation is from meeting the Standard.

In some larger organisations that have carried out this diagnosis, the above approaches have been complemented by bringing people together from throughout the organisation to discuss the indicators, or questions derived from them, in working groups, quality circles or problem solving teams.

Whatever approach is chosen it is important to involve a *real* cross-section of employees. This representative group may well include volunteers but it should not shy away from including critics and cynics as well. As well as getting a realistic analysis, involving people will start the process of gaining knowledge and understanding of what Investors in People is and how it will help the development of both individuals and the organisation. Also, the assessor will meet these people as a matter of course. The representative group of people should then become Investors in

People awareness-raisers and advocates, and spread knowledge and understanding. This is an important step, especially in larger organisations.

Deciding what needs to be done

Once the diagnosis is completed you will have a great deal of information about your organisation. Some of it will confirm what you already knew, some will be new to you but some may contradict what you had assumed. The latter may be the most painful to accept but it is probably the most useful information of all. If the diagnosis is carried out confidentially in a threat-free environment your people will tell you what actually happens, *not what they think you would like to hear*.

Most organisations have processes and systems that appear on the surface to be working but underneath, for a variety of reasons, they are not functioning as effectively as they should. These and a variety of other issues will present a challenge to senior managers in particular, but having this type of feedback also presents an opportunity to improve the effectiveness of the systems and people's perceptions of them and working relationships.

Although the Standard and its indicators are based on good practice it does not prescribe how things should be done, it merely describes what is needed. This allows the Standard to be met in the way that best suits an organisation. Fitness for purpose, in other words.

Of course every organisation is different, but experience has shown that in general the analysis will show that most of the information can be grouped under a number of broad headings probably including some or all of the following:

- communications;
- planning (strategic and/or short-term);
- systems and processes;
- management actions;
- monitoring and evaluation.

The information should be organised in a way that shows what is already working effectively, what could be improved and what is missing completely. The diagnosis and analysis should also take account of improvements that are already planned but perhaps not yet implemented, eg introduction of ISO 9000/BS5750, or reorganisation, delayering, re-engineering, and so on.

During this analytical and planning stage a number of organisations have found it useful to set up a project team. Again the temptation may be to include only line managers, but experience has shown that it is prudent to include a cross-section of people from different levels and functions; ideally they should include trade union representatives where they exist. The TUC recognises Investors in People, and local opposition or difficulty clearly raises a number of questions over the communication process. This will not only ensure that plans are practicable, it will also start the process of gaining commitment from the people. Experience has demonstrated that project teams can be equally effective in both large and small organisations.

Action planning

A plan should now be drawn up showing what actions are going to be taken to introduce new systems and processes and improve and maintain existing processes. The plan should account for any improvements already arranged, ie they should be integrated into the plan and not duplicated. The plan should stipulate who is responsible for taking the action and by what stage it should be completed. Ideally it should also be cross-referenced to the indicators.

A danger encountered by many companies at this stage is to let the indicators lead the action. One action may have repercussions on a number of indicators, therefore it is far more effective in terms of organisational efficiency to lead by actions. Certainly both large and small organisations have benefited in this way as illustrated in the case-studies. Once the actions are completed the indicators should automatically be met, provided, of course, that the initial diagnosis was accurate.

How long does it take?

Managers in every organisation at some time ask the question 'how long will the whole process take?' The plan of action will answer this question. It will also indicate the level of time commitment people will be expected to make. This commitment is likely to be the biggest investment of resources for most organisations. However for most organisations this extra commitment of time and resources should be reduced if the plan of action is developed in a way that integrates action to meet the Investors in People Standard with actions already planned.

The other potential cost, of course, is if the internal expertise is not there or available and an external consultant is brought in. Chapter 12 looks at the sources and roles and indeed the actual need for external help. For some organisations this is a source of concern.

Implementing the plan

Organisations that did not initially set up a project team to help develop a plan of action are advised to set one up now. The experience of organisations in our case-studies suggests that their role will be to:

- monitor progress towards achieving the plan;
- share the responsibility and the workload;
- share the ups and downs of the process in order to maintain progress;
- become the organisation's Investors in People 'champions', ie share information, encourage and influence colleagues;
- offer advice and answer questions (members of the project team will quickly become knowledgeable about the Standard and the indicators);
- bring information from the various parts of the organisation that show where the barriers exist and where things are working

effectively that will ultimately advise the group when the plan is achieved and the organisation is ready for assessment.

There is a set of informal 'golden rules' for implementing the action plan. These are:

- the leader of the project team should have 'clout' (ie there should be clear lines of executive accountability and authority);
- do not introduce things (especially paperwork) that do not help your organisation to improve its effectiveness;
- ensure you get commitment from those people who have to use the new systems and processes;
- keep things simple (ensure processes are designed in a way that meets what is needed as they will be easier to sell in order to get the above commitment and to motivate people to continue);
- challenge the traditional ways of doing things;
- persevere;
- be prepared for 'slippage' (most organisations do not meet their original timetable).

Gathering the proof

Chapter 6 explains what is needed in order to convince an independent assessor but it is essential that this is not left until the end of the implementation of the action plan. Throughout the diagnostic and implementation stages 'evidence' will be identified. It is easier to discard unnecessary evidence than to search for it at the end of the process. Our advice is have a 'bottom drawer' into which is thrown anything that may constitute proof of good practice. In most cases this proof will consist of extra copies of material such as forms, letters, reports and the like that occur naturally throughout the normal day-to-day running of the organisation. How this material should be sifted, sorted, constructed and presented to an assessor is dealt with in Chapter 6.

One organisation had an appraisal scheme that was not completed by all line managers. No action was taken against those managers who did not complete the process until Investors came along. Now Senior Managers want to know about any outstanding appraisals.

Summary

This chapter has illustrated the 'journey'. This journey towards becoming an Investor in People entails an examination at various levels of best practice emanating from organisations that have completed the process.

It has attempted to answer a number of the most common questions, such as

- 'how do we start?'
- 'how long will it take?'
- 'how much will it cost?'
- 'how can the bureaucracy be kept to a minimum?'

We have shown that there are potential benefits to be gained at *every stage* in the process and emphasised that the action being taken is to improve the organisation's effectiveness and not to meet the Investors in People Standard for its own sake.

CHAPTER 5

The Role of the Line Manager

Throughout the case-study section we refer to those people within organisations who take the lead in managing the journey towards recognition as 'champions'. (Even if, as is often the case, companies don't like the word, the function is still important.) A key role of these champions is to ensure that the process is fully understood and 'owned' by line managers and that they are equipped with the necessary support and development to enable them to perform this task to maximum effectiveness. This chapter, therefore, examines the important role the line manager has in helping organisations to achieve Investors in People status. It begins by examining who line managers are and how their role is changing, and looks at some potential barriers that may prevent them from effectively delivering their responsibilities. It then describes how this fits in with the Investors in People process and how the process can offer a framework to help managers and organisations.

Why a separate chapter?

A close examination of the Investors in People Standard and indicators reveals that only two of the indicators actually mention managers. This is deceptive. Organisations that have begun the journey towards Investors in People status and those that have completed it will testify to the significant part line managers play in helping an organisation to meet the Standard. For actual examples of this see the case-study section.

Alarm bells may ring in some organisations (and for many managers) that feel this looks like creating a great deal of extra work. If it does indeed produce a significant amount of extra work then some consideration may need to be given to evaluating the effectiveness of this role within the organisation. Experience suggests that additional work is generated only in those organisations where line managers are not effectively fulfilling the role they are paid to carry out.

Who is included?

The term line manager includes anyone who has responsibility for managing staff. It includes everyone from first line managers to the most senior person within the organisation.

The changing role of line managers

These are challenging times for many organisations. Increased competition, spiralling costs and a range of other factors conspire to create a fast moving and fast changing environment. Before examining the line manager's role within Investors in People it is worth looking at how line manager's roles are changing. Two strategies employed by organisations that impact significantly on the role of the line manager are delayering and decentralisation.

Delayering/flattening structures

By far the most common strategy involves organisations questioning the need for large numbers of managers at differing levels. There are many reasons for this happening but two factors stand out as major contributors to the development of the situation.

Firstly, the increased use of technology has made the gathering and utilisation of management information a far more refined process. Indeed, the sophistication of the activity is such that in many organisations the Tom Peters view that evaluation is the conversion of hindsight into management information is firmly built into everyday working practices.

Secondly, there is a clearly measurable trend to push more and more responsibility down the line. Whether or not it is Total Quality driven or cost led it is on the increase. As people accept this responsibility the need for as many managers disappears. In some organisations whole strata of managers have disappeared as staff have become more 'empowered' and have taken responsibility away from managers. Those managers that are left have a completely different role, facilitating and supporting staff rather than policing and managing staff. As we argue in Chapter 11, Learning to be a Learning Organisation, this is in line with the process of becoming a learning organisation, encouraging and enhancing empowerment, self-management and equity of access to training and development, backed up by evident cost effectiveness.

Decentralising the personnel and training and development functions

At the same time that layers of managers have disappeared a number of organisations have started to question the need for specialist departments to handle personnel and training matters. If responsibility is to be transferred as far down the organisation as possible, why not do the same with the personnel and training function? Theoretically, line managers always have had training-related responsibilities. Training, such as it was, was delivered with varying degrees of success. The existence of specialists within the organisation can quite clearly lead to a number of managers abdicating that particular responsibility in practice.

Training often tends to be 'menu' driven with managers selecting possibilities from a list of training courses prepared by the training department rather than engaging in a real in-depth analysis of what is really needed. Although this practice is changing there are still too many organisations who adopt this process. Departments tend to either organise training themselves or ask the training department to set it up. Indeed there is strong evidence from organisations of all types that real evaluation of the impact of training on quality of work and product is a real concern and a real weakness.

There has also been a focus on training as a separate or discrete activity rather than on development or learning on the job. An increasing number of organisations are developing complementary systems. On-the-job training deals with skills development, job knowledge and requirements relating to departmental priorities. Appraisal plays the key role in establishing these training needs. Meanwhile, a central facility deals with items of corporate importance and those areas such as team building where the skills for delivery cannot normally be expected to be found within departments. The strategic plan plays the key role in establishing these needs.

The manager's role in changing culture

So it has been established that many organisations and their managers are facing far-reaching change. The need also to change the culture of British organisations to enable them to meet global competition is often referred to.

Culture is often described as 'the way things are done around here'. Organisational culture is created by managers. For example management style will create a culture. If a manager is prescriptive and autocratic that will create one culture. At the other extreme weak and indecisive managers will create a different culture.

Numerous organisations have examined the Japanese organisational culture. However on closer examination there is clearly no one single Japanese culture, as for example, Toyota is quite different to Nissan.

So what is the answer and how can Investors in People help?

If the culture of an organisation is created by managers then managers must lead culture change. Investors in People again offers a framework based on good practice in people management. This however is not always readily seen. The model diagram Figure 5.1 shows a continuum along which organisations and people travel as their understanding of Investors in People develops.

Most people when they first look at the Investors in People Standard believe it is another initiative about training. Some reject it at this stage. Those who look at the indicators will see the word 'development' mentioned alongside 'training'. So it is not just about training but about development and therefore learning.

The next move along the continuum involves the biggest step. Until people actually apply the indicators to their own organisation it will be difficult to appreciate the implicit meaning of the indicators and the importance of the role and behaviour of line managers. The surveys mentioned in Chapter 4 highlighted the fact that managers and staff have differing perceptions. Does this mean managers need to behave differently? The answer of course is yes. The good practice in the Investors in People framework if applied will lead to managers behaving differently. Once this happens the culture will change and as can be seen from the examples in the case-study organisations, especially Uxbridge Magistrates' Court, effectiveness will increase. If behaviour and culture change in the right way organisations and their people will begin to seek improved ways of doing things. This ultimately must lead to a type of 'learning organisation' which will be examined further in Chapter 11.

The people at one end of the continuum who believe Investors in People is about training cannot understand why the people at the other end are getting so excited, almost evangelical. Those people at the other end don't understand why everyone is not as excited as they are. They have forgotten what they learnt by 'travelling the journey'.

To move along this continuum the authors believe people and organisations must apply the indicators to themselves. They will then *learn* about the important role managers should have.

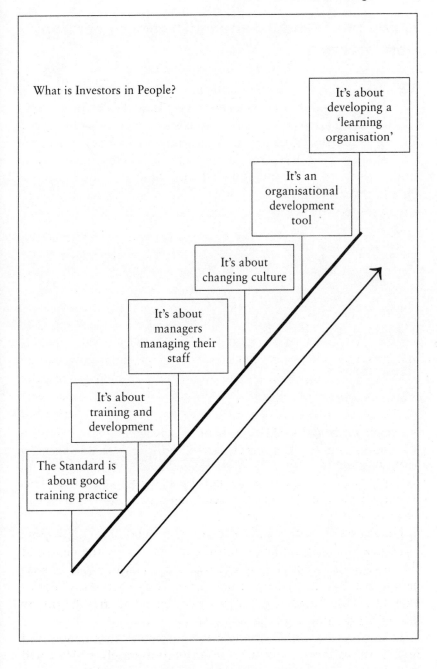

Figure 5.1 *Understanding Investors in People*

Using the Standard and indicators to develop best practice

We noted earlier that the Investors in People Standard is evidently based on good practice. This seems to be disputed by no one. Critics of Investors tend to focus on the inconsistencies of the Training and Enterprise Councils and the quality assurance processes rather than on Investors itself. If, therefore, this is the case, close examination and application of the Investors in People Standard and indicators should reveal what the good practice is and enable managers and organisations to identify what they need to do to train and develop staff.

There are four broad headings:

Planning
Ensuring that action takes place
Checking to see that action was effective
Communication

Planning

This involves:

- being clear about what needs to be achieved;
- understanding what knowledge and skills are needed to achieve it;
- reviewing what knowledge and skills already exist;
- planning to fill the gap between the two.

It is essential to ensure that there are sufficient resources in terms of time, people and money for delivery.

The planning process needs to happen on a regular, cyclical, basis to suit the needs of the organisation and the people within it. Organisations should also encourage and involve staff in identifying their own training and development needs to enable them to do their job.

Ensuring that action takes place

Once needs have been identified and action planned managers need to ensure that the action does actually take place. When the pressure is on, training and development can sometimes become a casualty, seemingly immediate items pushing it to the back of the priority queue. Managers must, however, ensure that training is not continually or habitually treated as a lesser priority. Before undertaking any training or developmental activity, managers also need to ensure that staff understand exactly what new things they are expected to do or to know *after* the activity has taken place. This may well mean having an informal discussion in advance to clarify aims and objectives. Throughout the process line managers should offer support and encouragement.

Checking to see that the action was effective

Following the completion of the activity the manager should check how successful it was. This should be done in two stages. The first is to check whether the person *believes* the activity has increased knowledge and skills; the second stage is to check after the person has had a chance to *apply* the knowledge and/or skill whether they are actually using them. The second stage is the actual and essential check on the effectiveness of training and/or development activity.

Communications

Throughout all the above stages communication should take place to ensure that staff understand:

- what the organisation is trying to achieve;
- how they themselves contribute to that success;
- who has responsibility for helping them to develop the skills and knowledge;
- that the organisation is committed to helping people to learn;
- and that they demonstrably share and celebrate successes.

The role of the senior manager

Senior managers usually have line responsibilities, so they have also to consider and respond to the responsibilities and expectations outlined in this chapter. In addition to these requirements, senior managers obviously have broader staff development responsibilities that necessarily encompass the whole organisation. In larger organisations in particular they will be involved in strategic policy development, ensuring that policy is understood and implemented, that value for money is achieved and that the benefits of training and developing people are clearly articulated and understood by all staff at all levels.

Some barriers that prevent line managers carrying out their responsibilities

Quite clearly in most organisations it is line managers, especially middle managers, that bear the brunt of the changes that take place. In compiling this book we took the opportunity to ask a range of these managers what factors prevent or hinder them from delivering their responsibilities in this area. Sample responses are listed below.

'Lack of time – too busy.'
'It's not the way we do things around here.'
'If I train my staff too well I'll lose them.'
'I haven't been trained to do it.'
'I don't see how it will help me to do my job.'
'This is just another management idea that will eventually go away.'

The majority have some sympathy with the notion that 'initiative overload' can (and often does) prevent them from doing their job properly.

Obviously if managers are to take on these responsibilities and discharge them effectively they are going to need persuading that there is something in it for them. They will need a lot of support from their line manager in the form of both moral support and offers of help to deliver and understand what needs to be done and how to do it. If they have not been properly trained to manage, appraise, coach and develop staff this will need to be addressed by the organisation as a matter of priority. Managers will need these skills and the organisation needs them to have them.

Managers will also need help to deal with the fact that developed staff are more threatening, more challenging and will probably have higher expectations for themselves and of their line manager. Managed, supported and developed properly, however, more able staff can actually make the job of a line manager easier.

Management qualifications and Investors in People

In 1987, a report produced by Handy, Constable and McCormack entitled *The Making of British Managers* compared the qualifications of British managers with their counterparts in Japan, Germany and the USA. The report showed that British managers were far less qualified. This report led to the creation of a movement which established the Management Charter Initiative (MCI), which initially toyed with idea of the concept of a 'Chartered Manager' but ended up with a set of management standards that managers should be encouraged to meet. An increasing number of organisations are examining MCI with a view to encouraging their own managers to demonstrate competence against the standards therein.

In 1993, MCI and Merseyside Training and Enterprise Council undertook an exercise that compared the requirements of the Management Standards and those of the Investors in People Standards. Not surprisingly there was a significant correlation between the two. A number of organisations that have met the Investors in People Standard have also used the Management Standards. (More information is available in the report: *Investors in People and the Management Standards*, available from MCI.) See also Chapter 12, Sources of Help.

Management development and Investors in People

Organisations that elect not to consider using the Management Standards will need to check whether their managers are sufficiently trained and developed in terms of skills and knowledge to support and deliver the requirements of Investors in People. There is considerable evidence emanating from the assessment of a number of organisations that managers have often failed to demonstrate appropriate competence and those organisations did not therefore meet the Investors in People Standard. Although there are invariably a range of reasons as to why an organisation is deemed to be not yet ready for recognition, it is most unlikely that one which has not got demonstrably effective line managers will meet the Investors in People Standard.

Summary

This chapter has examined how the role of the line manager is crucial in helping organisations to meet the Investors in People Standard. It has focused on some current issues and the skills and knowledge requirements of managers in managing and developing staff. These requirements are necessary in promoting a more effective, learning, organisation and for the achievement of Investors in People status.

CHAPTER **6**

The Assessment Process

This chapter examines the role of the assessor, what it is they look for and the nature and structure of the assessment process. It looks at methods of producing and presenting evidence to the assessor and what happens when the assessor visits your premises to interview staff. It examines the need for rigour during the assessment process while keeping the exercise as non-bureaucratic and as cost effective as possible.

The purpose of assessment

Some organisations, often the larger ones, question the logic of submitting themselves to external assessment. This may be because they are happy with their own training set-up or because the emphasis is – rightly – placed on the 'journey' rather than the 'destination'.

On the other hand TECs and their consultants will advise that if an organisation has spent a lot of time and effort in working towards the indicators, why not get the 'badge' to show what has been achieved. After all, external benchmarking does have some value in the market place.

It is the external benchmarking aspect that is the key here. 'If you do not bother to come forward for assessment how will you know whether or not you are as good as you say you are? More importantly, perhaps, how will your various stakeholders know that you are as good as you say you are?'

Toyota UK and Vauxhall Motors can be used as a good examples to illustrate this point. In the case of Toyota, for years they had been employing what they believed to be sound training and developmental processes, practices and procedures. They had been used as case-studies in numerous books and widely quoted as an example of good practice. They decided they would like to come forward for assessment. One of the main reasons they gave was to test themselves against the principles of the Investors in People Standard. That they met the requirements both vindicates the practices of Toyota and underlines the relevance of the Investors in People Standard in this context (see the relevant case studies).

The assessor's role

The role of the assessor is to check that there is evidence that the organisation meets the requirements of the Investors in People Standard and all the constituent indicators. This is done by ensuring that there are systems and processes in place, that they work in practice and the staff of the organisation are aware of them and agree that they work.

The assessor's role is to help the organisation to prove they meet the requirements. They should allow organisations every oppor-tunity to seek and present additional evidence, where it exists, at any time throughout the process. The emphasis is seen as being on encouragement rather than restriction.

Who are the assessors?

Assessors are generally drawn from two groups: staff from Training and Enterprise Councils and staff from training and development consultancies or units. To become an assessor it is necessary to have a background in training and development and an understanding of how business works. They have to follow a basic training course and then undertake certain developmental activities, to be granted and thereafter to retain their licences. These activities include shadowing an experienced assessor on an assessment, working with experienced advisers, and being shadowed by an experienced assessor when conducting their first assessment. There is provision for the quality assurance of individual assessment to be carried out locally as part of the quality assurance structure.

To elaborate further, on their first assessment they would be accompanied by a senior assessor – an experienced assessor who will evaluate the competence against Standards of the trainee assessor – and, in some cases, coach and develop as required. Once a trainee has 'demonstrated competence' they will be allowed to assess organisations unaccompanied but will need to provide further evidence to demonstrate their further competence against appropriate NVQ units in a range of situations.

To maintain their 'licence' to assess, assessors must carry out at least three assessments per year and submit to their assessment unit evidence of continuing professional development and competence every three years. They are expected to attend assessor meetings to share experiences and discuss difficult cases.

The assessment process

The process of assessment comprises the following stages.

- An assessor will be appointed by the Training and Enterprise Council or Assessment and Recognition Unit. The assessor will make contact with the organisation to arrange to pick up the portfolio of evidence (see below) and check dates for the site visit(s). Issues of authority and autonomy will also be examined at this stage (see Chapter 9). Some assessors at this stage may ask for a short tour of the site or ask to be talked through the portfolio by the person who compiled it.

- The assessor will then take the portfolio away and carry out a 'desk-top review' which will examine the evidence presented and compare it against the requirements of each indicator.
- After the desk-top review the assessor will be able to decide what the issues for discussion on site will be, who they will want to interview and whether any further evidence is needed.
- The selection of people for interview will be based on the factors shown in Figure 6.1, and will be chosen to give a representative cross-section. This is part of the scoping process and as well as some diagonal representation, ie not line manager with staff, evidential consideration must be given to gender, age, ethnicity and disability. A question often asked is 'how many people will be interviewed?' It is difficult to answer as the precise number or percentage of employees will vary from one organisation to another depending on the complexity and diversity of the organisation, its products and related functions. A general rule however is the smaller the organisation the higher the percentage of people selected. Investors in People UK have produced a guide for assessors and assessment units. This is reproduced as Appendix 4.
- The assessor will ask for a room to be allocated to carry out the interviews which must be carried out sensitively and confidentially. They will take place via a mixture of one-to-one interviews, group settings, and informal 'walkabouts' and in rest rooms, canteens etc.
- The assessor will decide who to interview but will generally leave it to the organisation to arrange matters in such a way as to avoid unnecessary disruption to the normal working practices. If shift working is in operation it is likely that the assessor will want to interview during the selected shifts.
- If the organisation employs people on different locations the assessor will also need to visit some or all of these locations.
- Following the completion of the site visits the assessor will then analyse the evidence, comparing it with the requirements of the

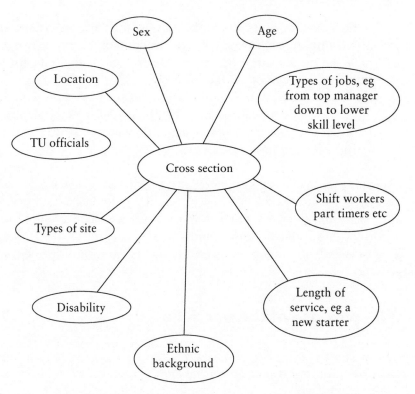

Figure 6.1 *The interviews: who do you include?*

indicators and, if satisfied that all are met, prepare a report to the Recognition Panel recommending that recognition as an Investor in People is awarded.

The next chapter describes the Recognition process. What happens when the assessor is not convinced that the organisation meets the standard is described later in this chapter.

What the assessor expects

When an organisation comes forward for assessment the assessor expects that the evidence gathered together will be presented in a way that enables the assessor to understand:

1. the organisation, its function, its structure and information about employees to assist with the selection of the interviewees;
2. how the organisation believes it meets each of the indicators that form the national Standard;
3. the logic and reasoning behind the evidence that is presented;
4. where to find evidence that is not presented (eg confidential material such as sensitive business information, items too big to include, and non-written evidence.)

Normally this evidence is presented in a ring binder which is referred to as a 'portfolio of evidence'. Those familiar with the NVQ process will have experienced portfolios of evidence. The amount of information supplied is important and great care needs to be taken to ensure that too much is not offered for reasons outlined below.

The purpose of the portfolio

Quite simply, the portfolio is prepared to demonstrate to the assessor how the organisation believes it meets the Investors in People Standard.
  A portfolio not prepared with the assessor and the assessment process in mind is likely to take longer to assess and may, therefore, cost the organisation more than would otherwise be necessary. It is essential to the ultimate effectiveness of the process that the organisation should not feel that the process is bureaucratic. Evidence should as far as possible be that which is 'naturally occurring' and has been generated for business purposes.

What should a portfolio contain?

Evidence that is:

1. current – it represents the current situation;
2. authentic – it should be proof of processes in place and not created for the purposes of Investors in People;

3. sufficient – volume is no substitute for quality or relevance. There are often one or two documents that demonstrate that a particular indicator has been met. Often one document may demonstrate how a number of indicators are met. If this is the case do not add extra documents unnecessarily;
4. clear/transparent – it should be self-evident why a particular piece of evidence supports the indicator(s); if not it should be explained.

A description of the organisation must be included – this will normally be in narrative form with a 'family tree' or an organisational chart. This helps the assessor to understand the organisation quickly.

A 'storyboard', ie a narrative describing how the evidence demonstrates that the Standard to be met is required. This may be done indicator by indicator, element by element or principle by principle. It should be cross-referenced with evidence in the portfolio or describe where evidence that is not included in the portfolio can be found. It can take the form of a matrix – evidence on one axis against the indicators on the other. As well as assisting the assessor and the assessment process, this is also a useful tool for the person who compiles the portfolio who can see at a glance those indicators that have not been evidenced.

The site visits

The purpose of the site visit(s) is for the assessor to check with the employees at all levels that what is described in the portfolio as happening does actually happen.

The assessor will ask questions to establish that:

* employees understand what the organisation is trying achieve and can see how their job contributes to its success;
* they have their training and development needs reviewed on a regular basis;
* action that has been identified actually takes place;

- discussion takes place to ensure that they know exactly what they are supposed to learn to do and that after the event they review how they are actually applying the new skill or knowledge, or take further action as appropriate;
- they feel valued and that there is a commitment from within the organisation to develop people.

Difficulties faced by assessors

The most common difficulty concerns the quality of the portfolio. The natural tendency for portfolio compilers is to put too much evidence in it. Sequential presentation is also important. As the assessor is comparing evidence against the indicators it is helpful to present the evidence cross-referenced against the indicators. As some details will provide evidence against several indicators cross-referencing will also avoid the need to duplicate evidence.

Where extracts from other documents are included it may not always be easy for the assessor to understand how the documentation works without an explanation. Some evidence may be self-evident to the person who selected it but it is not always so to an outsider.

The assessor needs to be able to understand how an organisation may have interpreted the requirements of the indicators differently. The standard allows this flexibility in order to meet differing business requirements or organisational cultures. Unless care has been taken in 'presenting' the case, an assessor may have difficulty with particular interpretations. For example, interpreting how training and development needs are identified in an educational establishment will be quite different to the methods employed in manufacturing. Business planning methodologies differ from one organisation to another, some do not refer to 'business' planning but to 'operational' planning or 'strategic development' planning, for example. Although assessors are expected to be able to handle these situations, a careful presentation of the evidence can speed up the process by clarification of meaning.

It is interesting to note that where development is 'on the job' people do not always recognise it as training or development and frequently have difficulty explaining how they acquired new skills or knowledge. Quite often they say they 'picked it up'. The assessor will try a number of approaches to identify where this occurs but organisations who use this approach to development should give the assessor sufficient information to enable them to check that it does actually happen.

Probably the most difficult decision that an assessor will face concerns those organisations who are borderline cases. The assessor needs to decide whether they are doing enough to meet the requirements of the Standard. The situations that cause most difficulty are when new systems have been introduced. The assessor has to check that they have been fully embedded into the everyday working practices of the organisation. The questions they ask themselves are:

'What would happen if these new systems were not used? Would staff object?' 'Would they notice?'
'What system existed previously?'
' If no previous system existed has the current system run a cycle and then been reviewed?'

Sometimes, especially in the case of evaluation, the systems are quite basic or even non-existent. In such a case the organisation may have to recognise that there are systems that need to be improved and developed. The assessor will need to judge whether what is in place currently is enough and whether they believe the organisation is committed to improving the processes.

Assessors, and recognition panels for that matter, do not expect perfection in organisations and their systems. However, some organisations may recognise that processes and systems could be improved upon. This should not prevent them from submitting evidence, provided it is adequate to meet the requirements of the indicators. It must be emphasised however, that plans which show that indicators will be met in the future are not sufficient to satisfy the indicators. There must be sufficient processes in place and working at the time of the assessment. (See Chapter 8, The Indicators Explained.)

What happens when the assessor is not convinced?

If the assessor, after giving the organisation every chance to provide sufficient evidence, is still not convinced that the requirements of every indicator have been satisfied, they will recommend that the assessment is deferred. In practice this would allow the organisation more time to provide additional evidence or take further action to satisfy the indicators. The length of a deferral will differ from one assessment to another depending on the pertinent issues. Some may merely take a couple of weeks to rectify but in the main the process will take a few months. When this happens the assessor will provide a report showing which indicators are not satisfied and present the report to the organisation with a representative of the Training and Enterprise Council in attendance. The TEC should then be able to offer and arrange support for the organisation to take the required action.

Deferred assessments do not normally go to the Recognition Panel. It is critical to the underpinning values of the Investors in People process that organisations are not made to feel that deferral is a failure. A lot of work will probably have been put into the process and quite clearly the organisation will be disappointed. Most organisations that have been deferred however have usually met most of the requirements and are therefore not 'failures'.

Because most organisations do not go public when they are deferred it is one area where statistics are somewhat vague and inconclusive, but a conservative estimate would suggest that about 20 per cent of organisations coming forward are deferred, some of which are household names and would clearly not wish to be considered 'failures'.

Summary

This chapter has examined the process and purpose of assessment. It has described good practice and highlighted the areas of difficulty assessors may be faced with. Finally, it has described what happens when organisations do not demonstrate that they have met the requirements of the Standard and its indicators.

CHAPTER 7

The Recognition Process

Why have a Recognition Panel? What purpose does it serve? This chapter examines the role of the panel and its function within the quality assurance process of Investors in People. It also runs through the structure of the Recognition Panel and the related recognition processes and activities. It describes who the recognition panel members are.

It also looks at the changes currently taking place in these quality assurance processes and anticipates how they may affect the future role of the Recognition Panel.

It will be of particular value to those approaching recognition or re-recognition, those seeking an overview of the process and to trainers and students.

Why have a Recognition Panel?

The previous chapter explained the assessment process and concluded with the assessor preparing a report to the Recognition Panel. Why can the assessor not make the decision? Why have a Recognition Panel? There are two clear answers:

1. It is an integral part of the quality assurance process to check that the assessor has done a good job and can convince the panel that the organisation does meet the Standard.
2. It has always been the intention that the decision to recognise organisations should be made by their peers.

Thus the role of the panel that Investors in People UK had set was to ensure that:

- all stages of the assessment have been properly carried out;
- satisfactory evidence has been provided to the assessor in support of all elements of the standard;
- the organisation is sufficiently free-standing as a business unit to be properly assessed;
- recognitions are consistent over time.

In other words, the panels exist to maintain the consistency and protect the integrity of both the Standard and the TEC.

Who sits on the Recognition Panel?

The precise membership of Recognition Panels varies from TEC to TEC but generally follows two models:

- a sub-committee made up of TEC Board members; or
- a committee of local employers to whom the TEC Board has delegated authority to recognise organisations. This committee will perhaps include senior personnel and training professionals but should be chaired by a TEC Board member.

As the number of recognitions has increased, most TECs have started to include among the membership of the Recognition Panel people who actually work for those companies that have gone through the process and are now recognised as Investors in People. A number of panels have included TEC employees who are also directors of the TEC. In future this practice is not likely to continue.

Panel members are unpaid and should be independent and impartial.

There are procedures in place to be triggered where there is a potential conflict of interest, such as a TEC Board member's company coming up for recognition, or an employer who has a contractual relationship with the TEC. In these cases the assessment and recognition process should be handled by another TEC.

Assessment units

In Scotland and in part of the East Midlands assessment and recognition arrangements have been different for some time. (As described later in this chapter, this model is increasingly being adopted elsewhere.)

Investors in People Scotland is a company limited by guarantee established to carry out assessments and arrange the recognition of Scottish organisations on behalf of Local Enterprise Companies, the Scottish equivalents of TECs. The Scottish Recognition Panels are held alternately in the Highlands and the Lowlands and are constituted in a similar manner to the TEC Recognition Panels.

Assessment East Midlands is another company limited by guarantee which was established by five of the East Midlands TECs, originally to manage their assessments, but now also manages the recognition process. They have a mixture of TEC Recognition Panels and a regional Recognition Panel again constituted in a similar way to other panels.

Arrangements in Northern Ireland

As mentioned in an earlier chapter there are no TECs (or LECs) in Northern Ireland where Investors in People is administered by the Training and Employment Agency. The Assessment and Recognition process however is very similar, with the Agency taking responsibility. There is a Northern Ireland Recognition Panel which again is constituted in a similar way with the decision to recognise being made by representatives of Northern Irish employing organisations.

The National Recognition Panel

A National Recognition Panel has been in existence since the inception of Investors in People. The original role of this panel was to recognise those national multi-sited organisations that chose to be assessed by National Assessors employed by Investors in People UK. In practice very few organisations have chosen this route, preferring to work with their local TEC. The National Assessors and the National Recognition Panel have, therefore, concentrated in the main on assessing and recognising TECs and LECs.

The national panel is constituted in a similar way to the regional ones, with its membership being drawn from the Board of Investors in People UK.

How does a panel work?

Assessment reports are circulated to panel members in time to allow them enough time for reading and preparation.

In the vast majority of panels the assessor is invited to present the report highlighting key information. Some panels ask assessors to use OHP slides but these are few in number. The assessor in a sense becomes an advocate for the organisation, arguing the case for recognition. This is especially significant in borderline cases. The panel will question the assessor about the assessment process. They will also seek justification that the organisation does meet all the indicators. It is important to note that they are not allowed to revisit the evidence so they are reliant on the assessor describing in general terms how certain indicators are met.

Following the questioning, the assessor will normally be asked to leave while panel members discuss the presentation and reach a decision. The chair of the panel will record the decision of the panel confirming that the TEC will liaise with the assessor on a date for feedback to the organisation.

Let's look at the process in more detail. The panel's role can be divided into four distinct but complementary sections :

Quality assurance
Dissemination of good practice
Maintaining momentum
Individual feedback

As mentioned in the previous chapter, it is the panel and the panel alone that has the authority to recognise an organisation as an Investor in People. The responsibilities of the assessor conclude with the examination of the evidence and the recommendation to the panel. There are currently no appeal procedures of any kind and the decision of the panel is final.

In order to ensure that the assessment has been properly carried out, the type of questions asked of the assessor by the panel will probably include some or all of the following:

- How did you choose the sample frame and why?
- Were you able to speak to all the people you wished to and if not, why not?
- What actions have you taken and are you planning to take to maintain the consistency of your assessments?

The last of these questions is set to grow in importance as the focus and of course the TEC funding moves from commitment to achievement. Panels will need to be able to demonstrate clearly to a wide and interested audience that there has been no diminution of quality. On the contrary, the additional quality assurance processes (see below) should be expected to demonstrate a genuine consistency of approach across the UK. Clearly the question of consistency has been raised several times in the context of the number and variety of TECs. The move towards linking adjacent TECs for assessment and recognition purposes will go some way to assuage this criticism.

In support of the aim of ensuring consistency, members of recognition panels must undertake specific training. Prior experience will be taken into account and panel members are advised to keep their notes to build up a portfolio. This is consistent with the general move towards competence based training. In addition, many Recognition Panels are also attended by a moderator, whose role includes, among other things, ensuring that the panel remains within its parameters.

The future

As the volume of assessments and recognitions grows the models described earlier seem to be the models for the future although a number of TECs still prefer to remain independent and continue to manage their own assessments and panels.

Henceforth, however, whether independent or not, Assessment and Recognition Units, as they are termed by Investors in People UK, have to satisfy stringent procedures. These include:

- sponsoring assessors (ie being responsible for their training and development and ensuring that they carry out the required number of assessments to maintain their licence to assess, and that they take part in meetings to share problems and discuss good practice);
- developing internal processes that assure the quality of assessments as they take place;
- internally verifying all assessments (this will involve ensuring that the assessor carries out the job effectively, and checking the quality of the report to the panel);
- managing recognition panels (ie inviting employers to become involved, and training and developing members);
- drawing up quality procedures that ensure that panel members have the reports on time, that panels are quorate etc.

Although these units exist primarily to recognise organisations they also have a broader role in supporting the delivery of Investors in People.

As the number of assessments increase and the panels see the same assessors over and over again, questions are being asked about the need for assessors to present reports in person to the panels every time. There are proposals that in future panels will read all reports but only see assessors in the following circumstances:

- the first report of a trainee assessor working under the supervision of a senior assessor;
- the first report of an approved assessor new to that panel;
- reports on all TEC and LEC board member companies, although with TECs it is already the case that they should go to a panel other than their own TEC.

In addition, Panel Chairs (and Internal Verifiers currently being introduced) should ensure that all assessors are seen an agreed minimum number of times. The role of the Internal Verifier is integral to the revised quality assurance process as the 'first line' checking of the assessment.

All these new arrangements will serve to enhance the credibility and rigour of the assessment and recognition process and maintain the national consistency of the Investors in People *National* Standard.

Summary

This chapter has examined the role and mechanics of the Recognition Panel. It has described the many types of Recognition Panels and their members. It has also anticipated future developments in their role and the overall quality assurance process.

CHAPTER 8

The Indicators Explained

In this chapter we examine the indicators. What is their purpose. How do they link with one another. Do they overlap? What will an assessor look for? Is there an audit trail through the indicators? The complete list of the indicators is included as Appendix 1.

For the purpose of this exercise the indicators have been grouped under a number of headings. Some appear under more than one heading. This helps to show how the indicators link together. One indicator, concerning continuous improvement, is new. As it is especially applicable to organisations who are due for re-assessment it is dealt with in both this chapter and in Chapter 10. Finally the issue of how much written evidence is needed is examined in an attempt to dispel the myth that the assessment is about bureaucracy

Looking at the indicators

To satisfy an assessor, evidence will need to be presented for each and every indicator. However, when working through the process of becoming an Investor in People it is necessary to look at the whole Standard. For this purpose the indicators can be grouped under five key elements:

- planning and monitoring for the organisation;
- planning and monitoring for teams and individuals;
- commitment and communications;
- action to train and develop staff;
- evaluating the effectiveness of the actions.

Planning and monitoring – for the organisation

The relevant indicators

1.2   Employees at all levels are aware of the broad aims or vision of the organisation

2.1   A written but flexible plan sets out the organisation's goals and targets.

2.2   A written plan identifies the organisation's training and development needs, and specifies what action will be taken to meet these needs.

2.3   Training and development needs are regularly reviewed against goals and targets at the organisation, team and individual level.

2.4   A written plan identifies the resources that will be used to meet training and development needs.

Purpose

This group of indicators sets the context both for the development of the organisation and the development of its people. Investors in People is about developing people to help achieve the organisation's goals and targets. It is not about having a large training budget, or always saying 'yes' to people's training requests. Training and development must be closely focused on the organisational needs now and into the near future.

Indicator 1.2 has been included here because developing the broad aims or vision is essential for the success of any organisation as the first part of the planning process.

The only indicators that must be demonstrated to the assessor as written evidence concern the planning process.

That does not mean that every organisation has to have detailed plans that analyse every eventuality but it should show clear goals and targets, measurable as much as possible, and the timescale over which they are to be achieved. Starting with measurable goals and targets provides the base for the monitoring and evaluation of organisational performance, and its importance cannot be over-emphasized. Some may be hard financial measures, others could be measured in terms of perhaps customer or employee satisfaction or reduced wastage rates. The question to ask is 'How do we know whether or not we are being successful? What should we be doing to improve?' You may find that a number of people in the organisation at all levels come up with different and valuable ideas when the questions is posed this simply.

The emphasis of Investors in People is always on 'fitness for purpose' so small organisations would not be expected to produce the depth of analysis and detail appropriate to larger organisations. However, they would be expected to take a longer term view even if this is only 12 months ahead. Larger organisations may have three or five year strategies.

Linked to this there should also be a plan that includes a 'people dimension' – identifying the broad skills and knowledge needed to achieve the organisation's objectives (indicator 2.2). There should be evidence that the resources (ie time, people, money and facilities) are there to ensure the 'people dimension' is achieved (2.4).

The plan should also allow for contingencies – sudden changes which may also affect the skills and knowledge required from people so more training and development, and perhaps resource, is needed to meet the revised targets (2.3).

This whole area of defining success criteria will become more important as organisations come up for re-assessment. If they have not got benchmarks against which to compare their performance how are they going to demonstrate continuing improvement?

What an assessor will look for

The first thing will be the vision or broad aims. Then the written plan, the targets and goals and how they link to the 'people dimension'. The assessor will look for evidence that the people plans are resourced. This is the start of an 'audit trail', which will produce evidence on evaluation. The assessor will also look for the links between achieving organisational goals and targets and training and development activities. He or she will look for evidence that progress is monitored and that the training and development needs of people are reconsidered where plans are changed.

Planning and monitoring – for teams and individuals

The relevant indicators

2.3   Training and development needs are regularly reviewed against goals and targets at the organisation, team and individual level.

2.5   Responsibility for training and developing employees is clearly identified and understood throughout the organisation, starting at the top.

2.6   Objectives are set for training and development actions at the organisation, team and individual level.

2.7   Where appropriate training and development objectives are linked to external standards, such as National Vocational Qualifications (NVQs) or Scottish Vocational Qualifications (SVQs) and units.

3.2   Managers are effective in carrying out their responsibilities for training and developing employees.

3.3   Managers are actively involved in supporting employees to meet their training and development needs.

3.4   All employees are made aware of the training and development opportunities open to them.

3.5   All employees are encouraged to help identify and meet their job-related training and development needs.

Purpose

This links with the chapter about the line manager's role.

The purpose of these indicators is to ensure that the skill, knowledge and attitudinal needs of teams and individuals are identified and taken into account by the plans of managers (team leaders, supervisors, etc). They also point to the need for managers to be competent. They demonstrate their competence in managing the training and development of their staff.

Again these link directly to the evaluation indicators associated with teams and individuals.

Indicator 2.7 encourages organisations and line managers to consider the benefits and use of external qualifications. Achieving qualifications rewards individual achievement and it will add to an organisation's credibility in terms of the skills and knowledge of staff in customers' eyes and provide an externally benchmarked measure of the organisation's 'stock' of competence and capability.

Amongst the external qualifications an assessor will expect organisations to have considered are National Vocational Qualifications (NVQs), or SVQs in Scotland, as well as appropriate national technical or professional certification.

What an assessor will look for

First the assessor will ensure that teams and individuals know who is responsible for their training and development (2.5). Then he or she will seek to establish how the needs of individuals and teams are identified and that *all* employees are included in the process (2.3). In some organisations this may be through an appraisal process or regular training needs analysis. In others it may be continual assessment and monitoring on the job against quality standards. Many organisations combine both methods using different approaches to suit the differing needs of the individuals and teams. The assessor will expect to see how individual needs link back to the needs of the organisation. It does not have to be an *appraisal* process but the outcomes should be adequately recorded so as to be effective over time.

The assessor will check that line managers have been trained and developed, that they are effective at developing their staff (3.2), and that they are demonstrating their competence by identifying these needs and creating a 'learning climate' for their teams (3.3), so that the teams and individuals also take some responsibility (3.5).

The assessor will expect line managers to agree with teams and individuals, through briefings and discussion prior to any activity, on what the training or development is for and how they will assess whether the training and developmental activities have been successful (2.6). Because identified action will not always require a formal training course but takes place on the job, the line manager has an essential role in supporting through encouragement and coaching (3.3) and in the provision of adequate time and resource. In short, the assessor will expect a similar kind of commitment from line managers that is expected from the top of the organisation to satisfy indicator 1.1.

The assessor will also look for evidence that managers, on behalf of the organisation, are encouraging the use of external qualifications, or at least have examined their relevance (2.7).

Commitment and communications

The relevant indicators

1.1 The commitment from top management to train and develop employees is communicated effectively throughout the organisation.

1.2 Employees at all levels are aware of the broad aims or vision of the organisation.

1.3 The organisation has considered what employees at all levels will contribute to the success of the organisation, and has communicated this effectively to them.

1.4 Where representative structures exist, communication takes place between management and representatives on the vision of the organisation's future and the contribution that employees (and their representatives) will make to its success.

2.5 Responsibility for training and developing employees is clearly identified and understood throughout the organisation, starting at the top.

3.4 All employees are made aware of the training and development opportunities open to them.

4.6 Top management's continuing commitment to training and developing employees is demonstrated to all employees.

Purpose

The purpose of these indicators is to ensure that all employees are aware of what the organisation is trying to achieve and how they can contribute to its success directly and through the enhancement of their skills. As well as being clear about their own role they should be confident that the organisation will equip them with the skills and knowledge necessary to carry out their role. The commitment to ensure this happens starts at the top of the organisation, by giving them an adequate priority to 'business' led training and development, in the face of other organisational priorities.

What an assessor will look for

Do people believe that senior people are committed to their training development? What does the senior team do to demonstrate its commitment – is it only in words or in actions and resources?

An assessor will expect to find evidence that communication to reinforce the requirements of the above indicators has taken place at all levels in the organisation. However, to add value, Investors in People also concentrates on effectiveness. Assessors will therefore be checking on employee understanding. This means that a great deal of the evidence for these indicators will be verbal – from the site interviews.

The assessor will therefore ask questions to establish how staff are kept informed about what is happening. Can they explain in simple terms what the organisation is trying to achieve and their part in helping that achievement? Are they clear about their own role and if not who to ask, especially if they need further training and development? How do they find out about training and development opportunities? When training and development is successful are they encouraged to develop further? What future training and development plans do the organisation have? How does this link to career development opportunities – lateral development as well as promotional.

Where there are employee representative structures such as Trade Unions, Staff Associations, Works Councils or other employee representative committees, the assessor will check how they are communicated with or consulted about the organisation's mission and performance and the provision of relevant training and development to support this.

This is the only indicator that can be omitted if it is not relevant because such structures do not exist.

Action taking place to train and develop staff

The relevant indicators

3.1 All new employees are introduced effectively to the organisation and all employees new to a job are given the training and development they need to do that job.
3.3 Managers are actively involved in supporting employees to meet their training and development needs.
3.5 All employees are encouraged to help identify and meet their job-related training and development needs.
3.6 Action takes place to meet the training and development needs of the individuals, teams, and the organisation.

Purpose

Quite simply, if action has been identified as being needed does it actually happen? Are new employees inducted effectively (3.1) to their job, the organisation, its environment and systems? Similarly, are those existing employees who change jobs inducted effectively to their new jobs? Do they get any initial training they need? Does action take place, in spite of other priorities, to achieve those skills and knowledge areas that were identified as necessary to meet the goals and targets of the business, and the needs of individuals (3.6)?

As mentioned earlier, because identified action will not always require a formal training course but takes place on the job, the line manager has an essential role in supporting through encouragement and coaching (3.3/3.5).

What an assessor will look for

Confirmation, either in writing or verbally, that the appropriate action has taken place.

Where they exist, assessors may ask to examine centrally held training records or individual learning records.

Evaluating effectiveness of the actions – the organisation

The relevant indicators

2.1   A written but flexible plan sets out the organisation's goals and targets.

2.2   A written plan identifies the organisation's training and development needs, and specifies what action will be taken to meet these needs.

2.3   Training and development needs are regularly reviewed against goals and targets at the organisation, team and individual level.

2.6   Objectives are set for training and development actions at the organisation, team and individual level.

3.6   Action takes place to meet the training and development needs of the individuals, teams, and the organisation.

4.1   The organisation evaluates the impact of training and development actions on knowledge, skills and attitude.

4.2   The organisation evaluates the impact of training and development actions on performance.

4.3   The organisation evaluates the contribution of training and development to the achievements of its goals and targets.

4.4   Top management understands the broad cost and benefits of training and developing employees.

4.5   Action takes place to implement improvements to training and development identified as a result of evaluation.

Purpose

As mentioned earlier the evaluation, 'audit trail' starts with the business goals and targets (2.1) and their link to the objectives set for training and development (2.2). These indicators ensure that these objectives are being achieved. This is what you hoped to achieve – did you?

Rationalising the effect and the benefits after the event is not effective evaluation! Nor are loose references to an overall improvement in general business performance or other organisational indices. It is also important to look at the processes and examine whether they can be improved, and if so, implement those improvements (4.5).

What assessors will look for

The assessors will look for evidence that the outcomes of the training and development is evaluated in terms of the learning that took place, and the direct effect on the business. It is not enough to describe the training activities and show business improvements without demonstrating the direct link between the two.

How were plans monitored? How were they changed? (2.3) How effective were the changes?

The assessor will follow an audit trail starting at the broad aims (2.2) and/or the objectives (2.6), how the resource was used, through the action evidence to the evaluation of the effectiveness of that action (4.1) and the impact on the business (4.2/4.3). This implies that you must be able to demonstrate evidence through at least one planning cycle from the identification of the business (or organisational) need, to the review at the end of the year (or possibly mid year) of the effect of training and development on the business performance.

The assessor will expect senior managers to be fully aware of both the cost and benefits of the investment in broad, but measurable, terms (4.4). In larger organisations this indicates that it is necessary for information to be collated from evaluation at team and individual level (see below) as well as at the organisational level to inform senior managers.

It is accepted that pure evaluation of the effect of training and development is almost impossible as there may be many other factors that contaminate results. Finally, the assessor will expect to see evidence from organisations that they evaluate the systems and processes and, where they can be improved and developed, that this evaluation is implemented.

Evaluating effectiveness of actions – teams and individuals

The relevant indicators

2.3   Training and development needs are regularly reviewed against goals and targets at the organisation, team and individual level.
2.6   Objectives are set for training and development actions at the organisation, team and individual level.
3.6   Action takes place to meet the training and development needs of the individuals, teams, and the organisation.
4.1   The organisation evaluates the impact of training and development actions on knowledge, skills and attitude.
4.2   The organisation evaluates the impact of training and development actions on performance.

Purpose

To check the effectiveness of the training and development actions on the performance of individuals and teams and identify areas for further improvement.

What the assessor will look for

This time the 'audit trail' starts in one of two places:

- the training and development objectives set at the identification of training needs (eg at appraisal or whatever other method is used to satisfy indicator 2.3); or
- at the pre-event briefing or discussion (2.6).

The assessor will check that line managers, team leaders, etc have clarified the purpose of the agreed action – ie what the person or team was expected to achieve (2.3/2.6).

Did the action take place (3.6), was it effective (4.1) and can they now do what was expected (4.2)?

The assessor will therefore also look for evidence of post-event debriefing to check what people think they can do, and subsequent evidence that line managers monitor the performance to check whether the training or development was successful.

The assessor will ask what happens if performance does not improve. Is further training or development planned?

Common weaknesses concerning evaluation

Lack of clear links back to organisational objectives

This is often caused by poorly constructed organisational objectives, eg they are vague and perhaps not timebound or measurable. Sometimes all objectives are not written down, eg a nursing home whose written business objectives are only concerned with refurbishment – were DIY skills needed by staff?

Sometimes evaluation evidence shows evaluation of the organisation's achievements and the outcomes of training and development but fails to make a direct link between the two. Quite often it is very difficult to follow the audit trail. An assessor should be able to start at any point on the audit trail and trace the links back and forth.

Not evaluating the outcomes of training and development

Quite often evidence is presented that shows pre-event briefings or discussions take place and post-event debriefings take place. What is missing is evidence showing how performance is monitored to check that the new skills or knowledge are being applied and are having the desired effect.

Sometimes managers say they are monitoring the effect but staff are unaware of it happening.

Senior managers understand the costs but not the benefits of training and development actions

This implies that expenditure on training and development has been an 'act of faith' and is bound to have an effect on the performance of the organisation, especially if it is very successful.

In some organisations, especially larger ones, line managers understand the benefits but senior managers don't, which implies that a method of collating information about the effectiveness of training and development is needed and this information should be fed up to senior managers.

The need for written evidence

The only indicators that must be met by written evidence are those concerned with planning (2.1, 2.2 and 2.4).

This immediately leads to the question 'just how much written evidence is needed?' Written evidence should be working documents that have been gathered together and that demonstrate that the indicators are met. Although most organisations will have quite a lot of 'naturally occurring' documents that can be used, relevant documentation will not always exist. However, the assessor will be able to question people in the organisation to obtain verbal evidence (see also the section on portfolio building in Chapter 6).

What is meant by 'all employees'?

This is increasingly important with the changing patterns of employment. At the least, you have responsibility to ensure that any one working for you under any arrangement has the knowledge to work safely on the site and to carry out the work required.

You would not normally be expected to provide development for self employed people or those employed by another who are contracted in because of their specialist knowledge or expertise. For example some college staff are contracted to teach their particular specialism for perhaps one session a week.

An assessor will not always look for complex systems to manage such people – again it's a question of 'fitness for purpose'. However, the assessor may elect to talk briefly to a sample of such people to confirm your explanation.

If you need further advice speak to someone at your local TEC (see Chapter 12, Sources of Help).

Summary

This chapter has examined the purpose and links between indicators. It has identified a number of audit trails that assessors will seek to follow. It has also highlighted some of the issues that will be important to demonstrate to assessors and illustrated some of the weaknesses concerning evaluation. Finally, it has tried to reassure readers about the volume of written evidence needed to satisfy an assessor – just enough is preferable to too much.

CHAPTER 9

Investors in People in Large and Multi-sited Organisations

The decision for large multi-sited organisations to work towards Investors in People status has proved much more complex than was originally anticipated. Although many organisations of this type adopt good practice, the size and scope of the organisation makes the process much more difficult to administer. Many believe they have adopted elements of good practice but fail to see what is in it for them. Others such as National Westminster Bank and Guardian Royal Exchange have made a commitment to work towards meeting the requirements of the National Standard.

This chapter examines some of the issues and offers some thoughts on how to proceed for such organisations.

The options

When deciding how to go forward there are a number of options for large and multi-sited organisations:

1. Work towards the Standard as a whole organisation.
2. Go forward on a site-by-site basis (or business unit by business unit). Provided each has the *autonomy* and the *authority*, each site or unit could be treated as a single organisation, work through the process and apply to be assessed by its local TEC.
3. Pilot the concept in a small, self-contained, autonomous part of the organisation. When choosing the part of the organisation to try it out it should be ensured that that part is representative of the whole organisation so that the lessons learnt are meaningful and can be applied to the remaining parts.

Autonomy and authority

The decision on how to proceed will involve examining a number of issues:

*   the degree of autonomy held by individual sites or business units;
*   the degree of similarity and disparity between the various facets of the business at each location, for example are they 'clones' like branches of the major retail chains such as Boots the Chemist or W.H. Smith Retail?
*   how centralised are the training and personnel functions?
*   if the organisation is part of a larger organisation does the remainder of the organisation have an Investors in People policy?

Guidelines

When choosing whether a site or business unit has sufficient autonomy the following criteria (as laid down by Investors in People UK (February 1995)) should be applied:

1. the site or business unit has a separate written, but flexible, plan that sets out business goals and targets which it has developed itself;

2. it devises and implements its own plan for the training and development of all those who work in the organisation and has the authority to change the plan;
3. it controls the resources (financial and other) which support training and development in the organisation.

The site or business unit should also be able to demonstrate three out of five of the following features typically associated with autonomous organisations:

1. it is a separate legal entity (or Agency status within Government);
2. it has separate financial and/or management accounts;
3. it has the power to hire and fire;
4. it has a branding and identity which is separate from any parent organisation;
5. it is the main focus of loyalty for its staff, as opposed to any parent organisation.

The issues of autonomy and authority have caused some concern and confusion. Investors in People UK are currently conducting a project. Further guidance will be issued to TECs/LECs soon.

Resource issues

It is also important for organisations of this type to consider the issue of working towards the Standard separately from being assessed against the Standard. It is quite possible to choose to work towards the standard in bite-size chunks and then be assessed as a whole. There may also be advantages in doing the opposite (for example a single, unified approach could lead to one portfolio of evidence provided it met the business requirements of the organisation.

Organisations that work towards the Standard on a site by site or business unit by business unit basis may be able to attract more financial support from TECs than if they went forward as a whole, although the amount of money available for support from TECs is becoming increasingly limited. The other advantage of going forward in smaller 'chunks' is that the more advanced parts of the organisation are not going to be held up by the less advanced; they can then become exemplars within the organisation. The danger of this approach however is that some parts of the organisation may be left out on a limb because they don't satisfy the autonomy rules and therefore cannot stand alone. The revised guidance is likely to encourage organisations to develop a strategy to take the whole organisation forward before any part is assessed. This should prevent isolated pockets being left out.

Although there may be some advantages to large and multi-sited organisations approaching the pre-assessment stages of the Investors in People process on a site by site (or business unit by business unit) basis, the implications for the assessment stage are that this approach will be much more expensive to the organisation as a whole. In this case each site or business unit would need to produce a portfolio of evidence and each site would be visited. Going forward for assessment as a whole organisation would involve just one portfolio and all sites may not need to be visited.

Whatever approach is agreed it is important that the organisation feels able to meet the standard in a way that suits its needs. However, when it comes to assessment the Standard must still be met.

Some examples of approaches by large organisations

A number of large organisations have already made policy decisions on how they should proceed with Investors in People and some have already been recognised.

Unilever

From the very early stages of Investors in People Unilever took an interest in its development through Trevor Thomas, then Director of Personnel, and a member of the NTTF subgroup. Consequently they took an early decision to encourage all individual sites within their business units such as Birds Eye Walls and Brooke Bond Foods to work with their local TEC and progress towards Investors in People status. Two of their companies – Elida Gibbs and Unilever Colworth Laboratories – were among the first 28 to be recognised. Since then most of their sites have achieved Investors in People status and the remainder are working towards it.

Interestingly, although the organisation decided to go site by site, representatives from individual units networked regularly to support one another and share best practice.

Grand Metropolitan

Like Unilever, Grand Metropolitan became involved with Investors in People at a very early stage. Sir Allen Sheppard (now Lord Sheppard) has often gone on record as being totally in favour of the aims of the initiative. Grand Metropolitan decided to approach Investors in People on a business unit by business unit basis. Some business units involved single sites, eg International Distillers and Vintners (who were also one of the first 28 recognised organisations) while others involved many sites, eg Burger King.

W.H. Smith Group

This is another example of a large organisation that decided to progress with Investors in People on a business unit by business unit basis.

Although at the time of recognition they employed 54,000 people, W.H. Smith Retail (ie the high street shops) have a strong corporate identity and centrally controlled Human Resource policy with each shop being a 'clone' of the other; the only variation being the size of the branches.

National Westminster Bank

The National Westminster Bank took a more cautious approach. National Westminster Bank Home Loans Division, based in Bristol, is a self-contained unit. They made a commitment to Avon TEC at a fairly early stage and the rest of the organisation sat back and watched with interest. In effect it was a pilot within the organisation and the fact that the whole of National Westminster Bank has now made a commitment to work towards Investors in People status indicates that the pilot was very successful.

Part Two: The Experiences

Introduction to the Case-studies

The organisations featured here have been selected to illustrate how the various stages in the process were tackled. They were chosen to represent a cross-section of organisations by size, sector, location and management philosophy. Some of them are household names. Others you may not have heard of. Nevertheless, they all have a common purpose: to develop their organisation by developing their people.

Most of the organisations featured have achieved recognition as an Investor in People. As we are discussing a continuous process, we include organisations who were at different stages of the journey towards recognition. This enables the reader to gain an insight into organisational decision making, action planning and implementation decisions as they take place.

Case Study I
Bedfordshire Training and Enterprise Council

The organisation

Bedfordshire Training and Enterprise Council opened, like many other TECs, in April 1991. As a new company with a £14.5 million turnover it had to establish its own identity as an organisation. The Investors in People process appeared to be extremely useful, as it offered an excellent means of addressing this issue. Accordingly the TEC launched its own Investors programme in October 1991, the same month that the initiative was launched nationally. (See Chapter 1, Origins and Development)

Moving on three years, the TEC again faced a massive challenge when it decided to apply in the first tranche of TECs seeking a three-year Operating Licence. All TECs must obtain a licence by 1998, if they are to continue to trade. Once again the process provided through Investors proved itself most useful in the work towards licensing. A licence was secured in November 1994, to become effective from April 1995.

Initial Investors activity was largely based upon the results of staff questionnaires, which confirmed the impression that the new TEC had of itself. There was no single TEC culture, owing in part to the employee profile. Some 60 per cent were seconded Civil Servants, who brought with them their own culture and at the same time, new staff were being recruited from industry and commerce, with differing values and behaviours. Analysis of a number of questions in the survey was of little value because of the existence of these two cultures.

Overall activity at the TEC rapidly increased and responsibilities broadened as new services came on stream, with a very considerable workload for all staff. This expansion of operation inevitably gave rise to a situation in which individuals lacked knowledge of the activities in different sections of the TEC. To counter this, a programme of staff briefings was introduced, which proved most effective in widening understanding.

In 1992 the Investors' Self Diagnostic staff questionnaire was used with the object of establishing an Investors benchmark, against which progress could be measured. As knowledge of what impacted upon the Investors process became better understood, it became clear that the organisation's culture was critical – in particular, relationships between managers and staff and in general, staff attitudes. Accordingly a comprehensive staff attitude survey was developed, including the original 1992 questions as a small but critical part.

This April 1993 survey then took over as the benchmark against which progress would be assessed. In addition, in areas where there were poor results, managers intervened to seek to overcome the apparent shortcomings. With hindsight it would have been far more useful to have undertaken the comprehensive attitude survey in 1992.

When the same comprehensive survey was repeated in April 1994, it showed improvement in most areas. The ball was decisively delivered back to staff at all levels. What were the specific problems in their teams, and how did they believe they could be resolved? This proved a most effective change in responsibility. Considerable and successful teamworking then followed.

It is important before we proceed to focus upon one important aspect of the 1993 survey results. The TEC recognised the fact that it had not been successful in getting the message across that Investors was not a quick fix and that there is of course 'no end to the journey of continuous improvement'. In essence, and of importance to all organisations going through the Investors in People process, they had succeeded in one particular area: raising expectations. People were more aware now and had been empowered to take a more detailed and informed look at practice and procedure, with predictable results.

In response to this and to the general view that people were not yet sufficiently empowered, working parties were set up, comprised of a mix of all departments, to work towards the development of a value statement for the TEC. The results went to the Board for approval and the Board suggested only minor amendments. Interestingly, and indicative of the progress that had been made with regard to ownership and empowerment, the working party considered the suggestion but in the main, secured agreement to their original ideas. Clearly this system was a powerful informal tool in getting the message across.

The agreed corporate value statement reads as follows.

Bedfordshire TEC believes that all people in an organisation are crucial to its success. The TEC aims to achieve a partnership between staff and clients that will fulfil their mutual needs and expectations.

We value . . .

- honesty in everything we do;
- a consistent and fair approach to decision making and policy implementation;
- the contribution of each individual;
- the effective use of everyone's time, energy and commitment.

We are committed to . . .

- assisting businesses and individuals to achieve their full potential;
- listening and responding to our customers' needs;
- ensuring wherever possible the highest levels of customer satisfaction;
- playing a leading role in the achievement of equal treatment irrespective of ethnic origin, religion, gender, marital status, age, sexual orientation or disability;
- respecting the time, priorities and responsibilities of others;
- encouraging, recognising and rewarding effort and achievement.

As so often seen throughout this book, the benefit is not so much in the resulting form of words, but rather in the process of getting there.

The value statement went to all staff and directors, and line managers had the brief of working with their team to identify ways of making it real in terms of their individual roles. Ownership had been achieved, now it needed constant reinforcement.

The original target date for Investors assessment was spring 1994. The pre-assessment survey indicated, however, that there were still several areas in need of attention, notably that the embedding of procedures had not yet fully taken place. A new target date of November 1994 was agreed. The strategy to encourage a more comprehensive employee 'buy in' of the values involved the linking of four complementary elements of corporate philosophy and commitments – the values, the mission, Investors in People and the three-year licensing process. The increased awareness of how everything linked together underpinned the need to improve communication still further.

In support of this, at the end of every Board meeting, all staff were invited in for a debriefing. After noting that not all employees felt comfortable asking questions in this environment, an additional clarification and question/answer function was required of line managers.

Other improvements set in train included:

- a system for grading jobs;
- a management performance system;
- moving still further away from a programme culture towards a more market oriented one.

To ensure impartiality Bedfordshire TEC were assessed by a National Assessor and in November 1994 they were recognised as an Investor in People.

It may seem like a long time, from 1992 to 1994 to obtain recognition. However, with so much else going on in the TEC, this is not too surprising. As a pointer to future improvements of the process, the TEC indicate the post-recognition feedback as an as yet under-exploited trigger for continuous quality improvement.

Case Study II
Thomas Bolton Ltd

The company

A consistently presented theme is that companies going for Investors in People status exhibit certain common characteristics. In this case study we look in some detail at a company who are just at the stage of making the commitment. Much has been written by TECs and Investors in People UK about those that have achieved recognition. We believe it would be helpful to organisations who are just starting out or are considering whether or not to go for Investors to see how and why that decision is arrived at.

The case-study is therefore in two parts (ie company profile and Investors in People). The first part presents a detailed company profile produced by Bolton itself. The second part examines the decisions leading up to commitment and the expectations the company has with regard to the potential benefits of the 'journey'. It is largely based on an interview with Ian Plummer, Managing Director of Bolton and their Investors 'champion'.

Company profile

A North Staffordshire company whose record of technical achievement stretches back to the early days of the Industrial

Revolution, Thomas Bolton Ltd is a world leader in the manufacture of specialist copper products.

Pioneers in the production of high conductivity copper using electrolytic processes, Bolton today is focused on supplying the electrical power distribution and rotating machine markets, with the aim of becoming the premier supplier in Europe. An aggressive export policy sees its products go much further, however, with customers in more than 30 countries relying on Bolton's high standards of quality and customer service.

The company nowadays concentrates on its well-known Boltomet range of coppers and copper alloys. Bolton's high conductivity copper comes in all shapes and sizes, as strip, busbar, rod, as commutator copper for DC motors and ring and rotor bars for AC motors, and machine parts. Bolton's components can be found in applications ranging from power stations and electric locomotives to domestic appliances – one recent high profile contract was the supply of contact wire for the Channel Tunnel.

Bolton also offers a range of high-tech copper alloys including copper chrome zirconium, copper nickel silicon, copper chromium, silver-bearing copper and sulphur copper as well as its standard HC copper range. Carbide dies are also produced.

Production processes on site are casting, forging and machining and additionally there are facilities for plating, brazing, hot rolling and cold rolling.

Process on site has been the target for significant investment in recent times. For example, the computer-controlled casting technology at Froghall is among the most up-to-date in the industry. Similar investment in the machined components department has paved the way to new products to satisfy customer demands.

Information systems within the factory have also been improved with great success, although expenditure was relatively modest. Now a shop floor data collection system, using barcodes on job order cards, feeds the very latest production information into the computer system for all departments to access and use – vital to the productivity of a company which has up to 750 orders in progress at any one time.

Quality and customer service are key issues in Bolton's strategy for the future too. 'We have long been regarded as a quality supplier, but our improvements in customer service in recent years are amongst our most significant,' said Managing Director Ian Plummer. 'We believe we are very customer friendly and are evolving partnership programmes with our key customers.'

BS5750 accredited, Bolton has received a string of awards for quality from both official bodies and key customers such as the French rail system SNCF and motor manufacturers Brush. Even safety levels on site have won a Gold Award from RoSPA.

That spirit of enterprise at Bolton is illustrated in the major turn-round of its export business. Faced with a much reduced home market, Bolton knew that its future lay abroad and so embarked upon a campaign to forge lasting links with export customers against sharp competition. The result has been a 75 per cent increase in exports in the space of three years. Particular attention has been focused on the Far East where recent successes have included winning an order to Japan against 'home' suppliers.

Technical development is an important feature of Bolton's operations. An example of the company's research expertise, and how this can be turned into commercial success, is Shape Memory Alloy. SMA is a unique metal which can return to its original shape after being deformed. Its rare properties are being put to use in a wide range of applications from fire ventilation systems to the antennae of portable telephones.

Specialist alloys is another field of successful product development by Bolton. Here sulphur copper and copper chrome zirconium are being used to produce welding rods and welding wheels which are attracting sales internationally. The contribution by all members of the 500-strong team has been an important part of the company's progress. Manufacturing across the site is being reorganised into a cell structure.

Recognising the importance of development in its workforce, Thomas Bolton Ltd has recently committed itself to a two-year Investors in People programme with Staffordshire TEC.

'We have achieved much, but we have even more plans for the future and both management and workforce are rising to the challenge. It's an exciting business to be in,' concluded Mr Plummer.

Why Investors in People?

Although in business for hundreds of years Bolton was in the process of decline for decades, the workforce reducing from 1800 people in the 1960s to 500 people currently. Poor financial performance in the late 1980s led to a major rationalisation exercise in 1989 to focus the business on the markets and product range they are now in. The company has a very clear coherent marketing customer base with a rational vertically integrated manufacturing process. They have a training manual which was launched in 1994. According to the Managing Director and Investors 'champion' Ian Plummer: 'One of the main reasons why we are going for Investors in People, is that we identified the lack of a coherent rational approach to training.'

There is an annual review for some 40 staff occupying a management role. 'We review the training needs of that person, but to be honest training for many was something we did when we could afford it and we didn't when we thought we couldn't and it was pretty informal.'

Formal training, in the main, consisted of induction training for new employees and health and safety training, together with an occasional longer-term course for a few individuals.

In terms of looking at a person's development needs and matching them with the company it was never really comprehensively done until recently. With the exception of one or two people in the middle management, Investors in People will be the first time we have addressed the issue properly. It marks a determination to manage training and development in a different way. I wouldn't say it was a cultural change exactly because we are approaching the culture we wish to establish anyway.

A four-year business plan was produced incorporating a mission statement launched when the product range was rationalised.

The mission statement was developed into eight key strategic objectives, the eighth focusing on the company's recognition of the importance of the people who are part of it. 'The only way we are ever going to be a success is if we can successfully tap into the potential in people.'

The eighth strategic objective is 'to continuously support and encourage all employees to add value to themselves and to the business using the most cost effective methods'.

The philosophy behind it is the recognition by Bolton of the fact that pressure is always there, on productivity levels, competition, size of workforce and so on. They are not frightened by the main current source of competition, emanating from mainland Europe, because:

> I think we'll find a way to compete with them and indeed serving a local market always gives you an advantage in this type of business. We're not expecting to be taken out of business by the emerging Far East either, but I think they'll give us a run for our money in 10 years' time. Therefore we've got to find more ways of operating smartly.

Ian Plummer is enthusiastic about the benefits expected from the Investors 'journey'. It is clear that he is the driving force behind the decision to commit. 'Doing nothing isn't an option for this company.'

The company is also realistic about the perils of perceived initiative overload and bedding new practices and procedures down where there are long established traditions in some quarters.

Bolton's have sought to blend new with old with some successes and sees the Investors process as offering considerable support here, especially with regard to preparing people to move up within the company.

> If it means going to night school, if it means being seconded to another company to get some outside experience, those are the sorts of thing we want to start doing under IiP. We should be giving people an opportunity to prove to us and themselves that they can contribute more. Certainly the sentiment is we've got to have a fundamental rethink. What I want to come up with is a full-blown manpower plan.

Ian Plummer believes that Investors in People gives them a framework to actually produce this plan with the added potential bonus of external consultant support.

In keeping with many of the case-studies and with the theme of this book, Bolton's are more focused on the benefits to be gained from the process than on any accolade Recognition may bring.

Getting the reward isn't actually what's important to us. What's important is that we go through the process, and we've already made a start, initiating such things as management development programmes, a survey of cellular manufacturing, and workshops for production managers.

The company will also take the opportunity to examine the relative merits of NVQs. They believe NVQs have both advantages and disadvantages and see the Investors process and the chance of TEC funding as excellent ways of testing out various ideas in support of the corporate view that the greatest skills of management revolve around facilitation and tapping potential, 'rather than telling people what to do'.

The survey undertaken prior to commitment indicated that the underlying culture at Bolton was a 'no fault' one. (In other words, getting it right the first time.) 'Customers pay salaries and wages, companies don't. I think people do care very much about customers in this company. We don't do it enough, but we do it a lot more than we used to.'

The company is not waiting for customer demand to lead them. Like so many of the organisations that have achieved or hope to achieve the Standard, they anticipate and plan accordingly.

We are launching partnership programmes. The purpose of our eight strategic objectives is to win business, not only by being cost-competitive but also by being pre-eminent in customer service by measurable means. We can have clear measures of our performance to our customers by developing partnership programmes with our key customers. This is to be achieved by continued management focus, employee participation, investment in manufacturing plant, and greater development assistance.

The company hopes to achieve recognition within 18 months for strategic reasons, because it's important for business and because the consultants have started to inform them that they have got elements of the indicators already in place.

'We have a clear communications plan, though implementation does not happen universally across the site, and we are going to address that.' Monthly cascade communication strategies will be improved. There is a three-monthly company newspaper and every six months the Managing Director gives a presentation. Also set for enhancement and development is the Works Council.

In conclusion, the importance of involvement of employees as much and as widely as possible is constantly stressed by TECs and consultants. Investors in People will not succeed if it is seen as a top-down initiative. This does not, of course, prevent senior managers from assuming the role of champion, quite the reverse: it can offer significant benefits in a range of ways. The senior manager will, however, need to be aware of this as is the case at Bolton's. A final word from Ian Plummer: 'We have done a lot in-company already. Investors in People will give us a framework and will allow us to do the gap analysis.'

Case Study III
The Frizzell Financial
Services Group

The organisation

Frizzell, the insurance and banking group with an independent financial planning arm, has been established for 72 years. Frizzell has a strong family tradition, considering its people to be its major asset. The company is based in Westbourne on the Bournemouth/Poole border on and around the 'Frizzell Roundabout' and it currently employs just over 2,000 people. In 1991 they considered the relative merits of seeking recognition as an Investor in People. At that time it was being advertised as the 'people version' of BS5750 complete with 'kite mark'.

Why Investors in People?

Following recommendations made by Tony Miller, their Head of Training and later champion for the Investors in People process in the organisation, Frizzell decided to proceed with Investors In People for three main reasons:

- staff related issues;
- organisational issues;
- impact on customers.

These themes and their subsequent development form the basis for this case-study.

Staff related themes

Frizzell decided that there were a number of ways in which Investors in People would benefit staff:

- staff would benefit from reinforcement of the view that they were part of a successful company;
- the external badge of quality would therefore boost an already positive self image;
- the survey promoted the sense of involvement and participation among staff and highlighted a number of areas for the company to address as part of its journey towards recognition.

Organisational issues

Organisationally, the benefits were seen as:

- getting the prestigious kite mark;
- giving a definite business advantage;
- helping with the development of 'people strategies'.

In particular these people strategies focused on staff appraisal and at better ways of communicating internally. An internal communications survey was undertaken, whose results triggered a number of significant changes:

- helping to maximise cost effectiveness with regard to training. (Frizzell's estimate of the total investment (£4,000) proved accurate);
- increasing positive publicity. Tony Miller takes up the story: 'We have been swamped with publicity since 1991 and have appeared not only in most of the national papers and

professional journals but also on television on a number of occasions and indeed in the Investors materials themselves';

- incorporating the additional dimension offered by the external audit elements of the process into planning and evaluation;
- introducing National Vocational Qualifications. (They did that independently of Investors in People but now the two are effectively linked);
- reviewing techniques and strategies of recording and evaluating training.

Impact on customers

Ninety per cent of Frizzell's customers are from areas that the company calls sponsor groups. These include the Civil Service, motoring associations, UNISON, the National Association of Teachers in Further and Higher Education, the Association of Head Teachers, the National Trust, and many others. They are nearly all national or local government related employees and a further benefit indirectly bestowed on Frizzell would of course be that they would be seen as supportive of government initiatives.

Frizzell was recognised on 17 September 1991, making them the first company in the UK to achieve the standard. Tony Miller again:

> There then followed a deluge of publicity and that was very good for the company. Also there is clear evidence that we have been successful in gaining contracts because of our status as an Investor in People. One contract in particular comes to mind, the Investor in People factor was valued as equating to a benefit of £150,000 which makes the £4,000 investment look rather small and insignificant by comparison – and that was just on one particular contract.

The company has been on television on two occasions and has been involved in a Europe-wide project which looks at best practice in training in Europe. Another initiative of a similar nature is currently under development.

The process

As is the case in so many companies, Frizzell note that at the outset links between the various elements of the Standard are somewhat difficult to see, but over the years the strands get woven so closely into the fabric of the business that it becomes almost impossible to determine where they are. The company see few if any positive aspects in the re-recognition process, and note that the cost was similar to that of recognition. Tony Miller recalls that:

> 110 people were interviewed, and I just wonder as to the wisdom of having a reassessment three years after the first one. I think if any company was not going to employ or use Investors in People properly it would be apparent after one year rather than three. It all depends on how you view Investors in People. It is the journey that really matters.

There are also concerns raised here as elsewhere as to the logic of the focus on commitment by the TECs and Investors in People UK. Changes currently being introduced making recognition the only real measure are welcome. 'It is like going to a Ford dealer and asking how many people have taken Ford pamphlets today and when they say "a thousand" you take that as meaning that a thousand people are interested in buying a Ford. The only real measure is how many cars actually leave the showroom sold.'

Also of concern was the fact that many organisations are displaying certificates saying that they were committed, with the question being raised as to how many of these actually convert to recognitions. The suggestion coming from this and a number of other recognised organisations is that it is an issue that Investors UK would do well to comment on at the very least.

The company is highly aware of the appropriateness of the development and introduction of Investors across Europe. Linked with NVQs and with a specific business-focused presentation concentrating on outputs, business opportunities become both extensive and attractive.

Benefits

The company credits its Investors experience and commitment with a range of factors including:

- significant business improvement since 1991;
- throughout the period of recession Frizzell has performed outstandingly in a very difficult market-place. This, the company believes, is a credit not only to the company but to the people-training. 'Our volume of training in the company is very high and so is our expenditure on training. It is interesting to reflect that in 1993 ten per cent of the 1992 post tax profits were spent in 1993 on training activities.'

The company feels that more could have been provided by Investors in People UK by way of guidance, especially suggestions for continuous innovation and improvement post-achievement of the Standard.

They also believe that the case is not effectively made for re-recognition on a three-yearly basis, save for the fact that the TECs sell it only as a 'good idea'. The Investors in People Awareness Week in October 1994 was a missed opportunity.

> There shouldn't be any interpretations of Investors in People by TECs and consultants. It's one standard. It always has been one standard. There ought to be assessors that are assessing the standard methodology. There ought to be fixed times for assessment and anybody employed in assessing ought to be able to stand up and give 20 reasons why IiP will help their business.

The company do not believe they would have done badly without Investors in People but it certainly has helped in a number of areas. Tony Miller notes that when the manager's survey was used in Europe 'we found to our horror that when asked "Do you understand what the mission statement and corporate strategy is?" 100 per cent of chief executive officers said yes they did, and 49 per cent of the next tier down said they knew it. This meant that 51 per cent said they did not know. So the questionnaire has got a tremendous strength of its own.'

Frizzell hold a number of accreditations as further evidence of their commitment to training and development. These include MCI, NEBS, RSA, BTEC and City and Guilds. They are an IPD Centre in their own right. They also believe that when applying for these accreditations having Investors in People has always been a help. For Frizzell, Investors is preferable to BS5750, 'which only tells you you've got processes in place. It's nothing more than that.'

Finally, in response to the suggestion made by several large organisations that they will wait until the customer demands Investors in People before they consider going for recognition, the company offers this advice:

You don't wait for the customer to insist, you surprise the customer with good service all the time otherwise you won't have a customer base to work with. That's what you should be trying to do. The British motorcycle industry might well have been waiting for the customer to demand electric starters on motorbikes. The Japanese weren't. Where is the British motorcycle industry today? Anticipate customer requests and demands and meet them before they arrive. Investors can help you to do this, and deciding to do it before it is demanded suggests you have a good chance of succeeding.

Case Study IV
Fujitsu Microelectronics
Durham Ltd

The organisation

Fujitsu Microelectronics, manufacturers of semiconductors, established production on a greenfield site at Newton Aycliffe, County Durham in 1991 and now employ around 500 people.

Why Investors in People?

The journey started in November 1992, when Jeff Thompson, the Training and Development Manager, attended a presentation organised on behalf of Country Durham TEC. He was not only impressed by the speaker but felt Investors in People would enhance what Fujitsu wanted to do. Jeff then needed to convince his MD and other colleagues. He saw that:

- they were already doing some of the things required;
- it would be a useful learning experience;
- it would be the catalyst to review and add focus to future investment in people;
- although there was lots of investment in people they were not evaluating it nor was there enough line involvement.

The process

An internal Project Manager was appointed, for whom the journey would be a useful development opportunity. She attended workshops organised by the TEC. She established a steering group within the Personnel Department to develop the processes and help to interpret how the Standard could be applied for Fujitsu, and offered her advice and support.

Apart from some guidance from the TEC they went through the process and achieved recognition without any external help.

The company realise now that if they were to go through the process again they would not have confined the steering group to Personnel staff as it was felt that they were too distant from the shop floor. They would have included a more representative selection of people from throughout the business which would have led to a more practical approach. This was seen as an important learning-point of potential value to other organisations going through the process.

The steering group looked at the TEC surveys/questionnaires and decided to develop and broaden the survey to cover other aspects, eg teamwork, how the company put itself across, and whether views were being listened to.

Early in 1993 all employees were briefed about Investors in People and told that there would shortly be a survey by letter and via team briefings. In May 1993 the questionnaires were issued to all employees (400 at the time) and a 40 per cent response rate was achieved.

Fujitsu's next learning-point was that if they were doing it again they would try to improve the way they communicated. They would have briefed employees in smaller groups which they believe would have improved the response rate.

Action planning

June 1993

The survey results showed a number of negative and positive points that led to the development of an action plan seeking:

- more involvement of managers in driving individual development;
- improved communications;
- improved evaluation, in particular following up the use of new skills and knowledge after the event;
- the need to have a broader-based development programme;
- the need for a formal training committee, made up of departmental managers, to increase the focus on training and organisational development.

It was also felt that they needed to demonstrate what they were actually doing to develop people. This committee met monthly at first but now meets quarterly. The action plan was agreed by the senior team and communicated to all managers.

As the process developed, other committees and working groups evolved. There were no dictates to line managers – in order to increase commitment a process involving influencing and persuading line managers was used. It was also decided that the portfolio of evidence would be gathered while the plan was being implemented. The profile of training and development increased with Jeff Thompson reporting to the directors twice a year.

September 1993

A second survey of about 25–30 people was carried out to measure progress.

Late October/early November 1993

A series of about 25–30 structured interviews were carried out to ensure that Fujitsu was ready for assessment: all employees were briefed in small groups and through a small note in the core brief about the assessment, combined with the opening of a learning resource centre.

November 1993

The assessment took place. 65 employees were interviewed in a mixture of group and individual interviews.

December 1993

Fujitsu was recognised by the Board of County Durham TEC as an Investor in People. The company reflects with hindsight that it could probably have got away with less disruption to production.

Outcomes

- Some existing systems such as appraisal were simplified and streamlined.
- Existing systems/processes were made to work more effectively.
- Management training and development were improved.
- The evaluation of internal training was tightened and strengthened. For example, the action plans from the existing Outward Bound course became more focused.
- Line managers became more involved in evaluation, for example pre- and post-event briefing and validation of the effectiveness of the activity.

Benefits

- Better internal recognition of what they were doing to develop people.
- Increased awareness of what other parts of the organisation were doing.
- Better focus through evaluation which has led to a better feel for what they are really trying to achieve through the investment

in people, ie improved training and education.

- Help in tightening up the induction process, especially the transfer from induction to starting the first job – this led to an immediate reduction in rejects.
- Overall, going through the process has helped increase understanding of why some tasks need to be done, this especially helps with non-routine jobs.

Since recognition

The Training Committee continues to meet but now it is twice a year. The steering group has been expanded to include practitioners. They have continued to try to improve the way things are done through continuous monitoring and review.

Case Study V
Monarch Aircraft
Engineering

The organisation

Monarch Aircraft Engineering was formed in 1967 and currently has 730 employees. It is part of an industry that demands strict adherence to standards, rapidity and flexibility of service, and closely defined internally and externally set and inspected quality standards. The company is part of Monarch Airlines and offers a facility providing full engineering services from basic turnaround and maintenance to full servicing of Monarch aircraft and those of a number of other airlines. It committed in February 1993 and was recognised as an Investor in People in May 1993.

Why Investors in People?

Although not initially keen, a mixture of pride in its in-house training facilities and programmes and a degree of tenacity by the Training and Enterprise Council led Monarch Aircraft Engineering to take up what by now had become the challenge of seeking recognition as an Investor in People. The challenge, simply, was to demonstrate by external benchmarking the veracity of its claims regarding the quality of its training and development programme.

This they did with some style, becoming the fastest organisation to be recognised, taking just under three months in the process. Monarch's champion, Director of Personnel Julie Bonner, takes up the story.

> Once the local TEC's challenge had been taken up and we had agreed to demonstrate via external assessment our commitment to training and development, we learned that some of our assumptions about Investors were not entirely accurate. For instance, it was generally thought that the process was excessively bureaucratic. It isn't. We also negotiated with the TEC to use the services of a consultant of our own choice who had worked with us for some time previously. This was readily agreed and meant that we hit the ground running, so to speak, as the consultant already had a good picture of the structure and culture of the organisation. Incidentally, the consultant was funded and trained by the TEC and later was successful in gaining employment with them. We regard this as an excellent example of a 'by product' of Investors in People.

Monarch expected to have no difficulty in putting the storyboard together and this proved to be the case. Julie Bonner again: 'We certainly had no real problems with assembling the evidence. Given the highly regulated nature of the business it would be a surprise and a real cause for concern if this were the case!'

Monarch does not believe the Investors in People process has altered the organisation tremendously, but is firmly convinced that it has conferred a range of 'pluses'. The main benefits of the journey as perceived by Monarch are summarised below.

- It enabled clarification and communication of business objectives. Here the opportunity was taken to raise internal awareness of the company, its objectives, its customer profile and so on. This was done partly by the production of special editions of the in-house magazine. Information about going for Investors in People was done in tandem with this.
- Employees were encouraged to examine their particular role and its contribution to departmental and organisational goals. There was a special focus on administrative and clerical staff who previously had been neglected in terms of training. The appraisal process for this group of employees was reviewed and enhanced.

Outcomes of not include improved motivation among this group and an increased sense of job value.

- Following the focus on time spent on training, the knowledge thus gained led to greater efficiency in the distribution and quantity of training – 'the right training at the right time'.
- Improvements have been made to the induction process with a greater emphasis placed on the role of the line manager as part of the overall strategy for new staff.
- Of particular interest, perhaps, is Monarch's commitment to self-appraisal. Here the engineer ranks his or her own skills prior to the appraisal interview where these rankings are then discussed. The company has found this to be an effective mechanism in so far as staff tend to be more critical of themselves than their line managers are – giving all concerned something of a morale boost!
- Since recognition, a clear focus on 'the background boys and girls' has remained a feature as Monarch keeps the initiative rolling.

Few if any minus points were attached to the process by Monarch, whose stated wish of wanting to emphasise the importance of people was clearly enhanced by its Investors in People journey. Monarch found the assessment process to be rigorous and the post recognition debriefing to be positive, constructive and sensitive.

Finally, it is worth noting that in Monarch's view, and in contrast to much 'received wisdom', cynicism and scepticism had been less evident in the workforce than within management!

Case Study VI
The University of Luton and
The Open University

The case-study on Investors in People in Higher Education is a comparative one and focuses on two universities. The first, the University of Luton, is currently England's newest university and became the first in the UK to achieve the Standard, in April 1994. The second, the Open University, is the largest university in the UK, with some 11,000 staff. The Open Business School achieved recognition in December 1994 and the rest is progressing towards recognition in 1995.

This case-study draws significantly on 'Learning to be a Learning Organisation' by Heather Hamblin of the Open Business School and Bob Thackwray. We would like to thank Heather for her kind permission to use material from the article.

The organisation

The University of Luton was granted university status on 14 July 1993. Luton was the first, and remains the only, institution to have been directly designated a university under stringent new procedures and criteria. It currently has over 1,100 staff and 13,000 students who attend on full and part time bases. There is a strong local and regional commitment but in addition students are drawn from all over the UK and overseas. The university is committed to education and training that has a particular relevance to work and employment. It therefore boasts strengths in such areas as technology, construction, science, computing, business and management.

The Open University launched its first post-experience distance learning courses in management in 1983, through its registered trade name the Open Business School which was then a very small Management Education section with only a handful of staff within Continuing Education. Since October 1983 there have been some 100,000 registrations of practising managers on Open Business School courses, and from 1 January 1988 the University designated the Open Business School as the School of Management with full faculty status to act as a focus for teaching and research in management studies. Since 1994 the Open Business School has offered a three-tier system of qualifications – Certificate, Diploma and Master's in Business Administration – in the UK and in continental western and eastern Europe. It has some 20,000 student registrations a year, and now some 140 staff (including its representatives in the university's 13 UK regional centres).

The University of Luton

The management of change had been the abiding theme over the past few years as the institution focused its corporate energy on achieving polytechnic, then university status. As the institution grew and its role matured, three significant factors emerged.

1. The qualitative aspects of human resource management had to feature even more prominently than the quantitative.
2. Adding value to current staff and the recruitment and retention of new staff must both continue as high profile activities.
3. Much greater corporate effort will need to be invested in more effective communication, consultation and team-building.

It was the process of implementing actions in support of achieving the third point that saw the then Luton College of Higher Education commit itself in October 1992 to becoming an Investor in People. In particular, attention had to be paid to the position of administrative, clerical, technical and other support staff with regard to their personal professional development. It was also clear that a significant degree of teamwork, and the development of related skills in support of this, would be necessary to secure university status. The teamwork element, and the need to bring together a range of seemingly unrelated initiatives, made Investors in People seem increasingly appropriate to the organisation.

It was essential to seek much greater involvement of all categories of employee. The potential gains were clear – the development of a more coherent framework for addressing the professional development requirements of support and technical staff. The newly created (1992) Centre for Educational Development sought to address the personal and professional development challenge and the newly introduced Career Review process was created to support the process of identification of training needs for all categories of employee. Investors in People, therefore, was seen to provide an appropriate Total Quality vehicle to assist in identifying and removing the barriers between academic and support staff.

Like the rest of higher education the institution had gone through unparalleled development and expansion. Less than one year after making the commitment to become an Investor in People, on 14 July 1993, the Privy Council granted the institution the authority to be called the University of Luton. The Order was the culmination of an intensive period of rigorous external scrutiny by the Council for National Academic Awards and the Higher Education Quality Council, involving all employees at all levels in an achievement which remains unique in UK higher education.

The management of change, therefore, is of paramount importance. In common with other universities, Luton has a culture that differs from that found in other sectors of employment; this culture relates to the nature of higher education, and is reflected in the university's organisational arrangements. On the one hand, it is the university's expectation that all staff will regard the interests of its students as paramount, and will implement institutional policies which sustain the quality of students' learning experience; on the other hand, the academic members of staff have an equally strong loyalty to their subject, and for this purpose perceive their reference group as being staff from a similar disciplinary background employed in other institutions or in professional practice, and not their immediate colleagues at Luton. This dual loyalty on the part of academic staff, which is manifested in the slightly different structural arrangements for academic leadership and line management, leads to a healthy creative tension in the university, and means that change has to be justified, not imposed. It also means that a key task of management is to create the conditions under which the direction of development is accepted and policy is owned, often entailing lengthy discussions through the committee structure of the university. This introduces the other significant feature of life at the university: that because it is an intrinsic part of being an academic to be sceptical and critical, and because all knowledge and judgements are in principle changeable, academic policies and judgements are formed collectively by groups of staff rather than by individuals. In effect, the Investors in People process was questioned and examined at every stage. In terms of the organisation's culture this was entirely appropriate.

Another significant feature of the university is the extent to which its development is influenced by the views of its stakeholders. They include:

- students;
- employers (in their roles as employers of graduates, providers of workplace experience for students, commissioners of short courses, research and consultancy, and sponsors of students on part-time courses);
- the Government (principally the Department for Education and the Department of Employment);
- the Higher Education Funding Council for England (which allocates public funds to the University and assesses the quality of education it provides;
- the Higher Education Quality Council (which audits the university's quality assurance systems);
- national validating/accrediting bodies (for example the Business and Technology Education Council, the National Council for Vocational Qualification, and the various professional institutions).

Other influential views are provided by the university's external examiners and moderators, and by the various external advisers it employs to assist in developing and sustaining courses and research of high quality. The successful operation of the university entails constant monitoring and evaluation of its activities in two critical phases.

- The information and advice received from stakeholders has to be evaluated at the point of receipt, to determine its precise applicability to the mission and development of the university.
- The university's courses and research activities have to be evaluated at the point of delivery, to ensure that they are consistent with the legitimate expectations of its stakeholders.

External influence and benchmarking is therefore an integral and routine part of the university's work. From an Investors in People perspective, this has three major advantages.

- The effectiveness of training and development plans is constantly being assessed by bodies and individuals external to the university.
- This constant contact with outside views invigorates the working environment of individual members of staff and is in itself a very significant staff development opportunity.
- Stakeholders' comments will contribute to the university's training and development needs analysis.

The Open University and its Open Business School

At the Open University the impetus to adopt a formal performance/ quality scheme partly began in the Open Business School (OBS), which in 1992 believed that some of its larger corporate clients, who sponsored large numbers of their employees to take OBS courses, might soon require BS5750 of all suppliers. At the same time the OU's Business Development and Marketing Office began to proselytise for the Total Quality Management approach and TQM seminars were attended by a cross-section of the OU staff. This happened at a time when the OU was preparing its first draft of *Plans for Change: the University's Strategic and Development Plans*, for the next ten-year period. It itemises six key 'new directions' for change by the university which underpin all its future development initiatives.

The University was making good progress in implementing the formally agreed Career Development and Staff Appraisal (CDSA) processes and providing training at various levels. In this situation the OU's leadership was concerned that 'initiative fatigue' could easily set in if each of these were to be tackled separately. No formal performance/quality improvement scheme could be entertained unless it actually reduced the number of initiatives by fusing some of them together.

The Investors in People programme seemed to have the potential to integrate many of these change processes in that it provided a format for developing these business plans by working from university through to relevant unit objectives which put these into practice. Further encouragement came from a survey of the Open Business School's corporate clients. When asked whether they would like their suppliers to implement BS5750, Investors in People or TQM, Investors in People was by a narrow margin the most popular choice. Therefore, a number of factors contributed to the OU's decision to make a general commitment to it in April 1993: Investors in People

- seemed more appropriate to an educational institution than BS5750, which was originally conceived for the manufacturing industry;
- had a clear and external assessment process in contrast to the more subjective judgements inherent in TQM;
- had a non-threatening title (some university staff complain of creeping managerialism in higher education);
- focused on developing people (this was especially appropriate to a knowledge-based enterprise like a university);
- emphasised the importance of business planning;
- provided a formal framework for checking that all staff had the

skills and awareness needed to contribute to strategic change over the coming years;
- encouraged the uptake of NVQs;
- was not intended to be a once-and-for-all process.

In the summer of 1993 both the OU Educational Enterprises (OUEE) unit and the OU's Open Business School made their separate public commitments to each become an Investor in People. These two units would act as pilot projects for the rest of the university to be introduced to Investors in People in 'waves' from 1994 onwards, with the aim of being ready to apply together for the Investors in People standard in 1996. Members of an Investors Steering Group and a project team are visiting each unit to help them prepare and implement their own action plan. Other units will also be able to learn from the experiences of OUEE and the Open Business School.

The two experiences compared

Both universities became involved in Investors in People because of a wider interest on the parts of the respective top teams in Total Quality Management (TQM) and how this could effectively be taken on board within their respective domains of the higher education sector. For both, this interest in Investors in People coincided with other external and internal influences which had demanded, or were requiring, organisational change on several fronts. Luton College of Higher Education (as it then was) committed to Investors in People as a way of building further on significant successful changes already taking place, notably the granting of its own taught degree accreditation – the first stage towards its achieving independent university status. 'The team spirit at the time' and the sense of all working together towards this common goal were recognised as tangible outcomes of gaining this accreditation and Investors in People was seen as a timely and very opportune way to capitalise on this.

The Open Business School adopted the pursuit of Investors in People as a valuable tool at a particular stage in this young Faculty's growth and development. On 1 April 1993 the school's first elected Dean commenced his three-year term of office and headed up a new management structure for the school which had been devised and approved by all members of the faculty after a time-consuming but highly consultative process. It was considered that now was the time to take a lead in the impetus for Investors in People, partly emanating from the university's top management, as well as from within the school itself, and for the Business School to address certain human resource issues head-on which, until that time, had been somewhat neglected. Whereas Luton had seen it as important that the total organisation commit to, and pursue, Investors in People together, the Open Business School therefore 'volunteered' to be one of two initial Investors in People pilots after which the rest of the Open University would work towards gaining the award in 1996.

Conclusions

Neither the University of Luton nor the Open Business School experienced Investors in People as being primarily driven by a central university personnel or human resource unit. However Luton employed Investors in People as a vehicle to address and resolve ongoing human resource issues (such as, among others, better communications, the position of part-time staff, to improve induction and embed career review, particularly for support staff), and the Open Business School used Investors in People as a framework on which to develop and build competency-based human resource management within the school.

Both organisations utilised the services of an external consultant for some specific parts of the process but by far the greatest emphasis within the implementation strategies adopted by both organisations was placed on structured, participative consultation. This embraced all levels and categories of staff over a protracted period of some six to twelve months and was co-ordinated by an internal Investors' group (Luton) or a representative steering group (Open Business School). This consultation took the form, within Luton, of awareness seminars for all staff, heads of departments addressing their team (staff) meetings and 'every single decision-making body in the institution having it on its agenda at least once and probably several more times'. Within the Open Business School, the consultation took the form of agreeing competences within the respective staff groupings, a school-wide seminar, Investors in People being a regular item on School Board and the faculty's management committee's agendas and in-depth focus groups for all staff. In addition the internal communication channels were well utilised to inform and update as to progress towards Investors in People, such as the University-wide publications 'The Flag' and 'News Briefing' (Luton) and the weekly E-mail 'Friday Newsletter' and four-monthly 'Investors in People News' (Open Business School), which reached all staff. External consultants undertook an attitude survey across all staff (Open Business School) or a randomly selected desktop review with follow-up interviews of some staff (Luton) in the early stages of Investors in People – before formal committal for the Open Business School but post-dating it in the case of Luton. This survey was to ascertain the existing training and development climate within the respective organisations, as recommended in the national guidelines. Both then formulated their respective action plans incorporating their response to this valuable employee feedback. In both cases these action plans were adapted and amended several times along the journey. Neither Luton nor the Open Business School undertook a 'mock' assessment prior to the formal assessment. Reasons for this were varied but tended to reflect the feeling that there was a wealth of recent experience in dealing with inspection, audit and assessment (in relation to recognition as a university in the case of Luton, and the HEFCE and AMBA visits at the Open Business School) and a rehearsal would be viewed as unnecessary and counter-productive.

After some initial assistance from the respective Training and Enterprise Councils, both organisations sank some part of their own financial resources and considerable staff time, particularly in the form of the central co-ordinating groups, into implementing and progressing Investors in People.

Both institutions found that Investors in People did help considerably to sharpen the focus on overall 'business objectives' and they noted how these cascaded down into more meaningful, localised, shorter and longer term objectives for the respective 'business units' (faculties and departments at Luton and the Open Business School itself). All these 'shared visions' were widely communicated to all staff. Investors in People also served to raise the issue of what is meant by effective 'line management' in the changing political and economic climate surrounding these higher education institutions in the 1990s; and for both, Investors in People certainly embedded better management practices in respect of their human resources, and somewhat faster than might have been achieved otherwise.

Case Study VII
Ramada Hotel Heathrow

The organisation

The Ramada Hotel Heathrow is one of four Ramada Hotels in the UK, the others being at Gatwick, Manchester and Reading, and is controlled by Ramada International Hotels and Resorts which has 138 hotels worldwide. This hotel has 638 bedrooms and employs 230 staff. Ramada took over its management in January 1993; prior to that it was known as the Heathrow Penta.

The group of hotels became interested in Investors in People in early 1994 and undertook a diagnostic exercise in June of that year. The diagnosis showed that the hotels had quite different structures and were likely to go forward at different rates. They decided therefore to work towards the Investors in People Standard independently, although they do liaise with one another.

Reasons for making the commitment

Following the change from Heathrow Penta to Ramada Hotel there was a need to change the culture, introduce flexible working practices and encourage staff to become more involved. Investors in People was seen as the tool to help this come about. It also displayed:

- a black and white commitment to looking after staff;
- a commitment to both guests and customers;
- a number of PR benefits which were expected as an end result.

The approach

Feeling that they did not want to pay lip-service to the process, the approach adopted by the Ramada Heathrow had been to involve all heads of department from the start. This involved the heads meeting to learn what Investors in People was all about, seeking their commitment, and brainstorming ideas about the way forward.

They decided to produce action plans department by department. These have been produced by involving all staff in the planning process. The action plans are based on the answers to three questions:

- Where are we now?
- Where do we want to be?
- How will we get there?

The General Manager of the hotel is also thoroughly involved in this process and each Monday a head of department is invited to report progress.

The Human Resources Department sees its job as facilitating the process which is led and owned by heads of department. Action plans are devised and examined and these have led to a range of training and development activities, with an enormous number of ideas for improvements to the service offered to customers, all of them generated by employees. The Department looks for areas where needs are common and meets those needs on a hotel-wide basis. Among the issues, prioritising, statutory, mandatory, customer care, management development, core skills, computer literacy, on-job training have become focal points.

The hotel created a training room as an immediate benefit. Almost immediately there was a definite buzz about the place. Investors posters were displayed throughout the hotel to keep the subject in people's minds. Everybody got involved and took the opportunity to contribute towards Investors in People. They have had a lot of help, particularly in the form of workshops from West London TEC.

The main issues that the hotel faced concerned managing the varying degrees of enthusiasm and commitment from the heads of department. Initially this led to one department leaping forward so fast that the others were somewhat left behind. Asking their department to hold back may have affected their enthusiasm but did not lead to a lessening of commitment. Gradually all the other departments caught up.

However in July 1995 some doubts started to emerge whether the target date of September 1995 for assessment would be met. It was decided to re-run the original survey, similar to the one in appendix of this book. The survey results indicated that the hotel met the requirements of the Standard but it was the replies to an additional question that was asked that really convinced the General Manager that the hotel was ready for assessment. The additional question and the responses are shown below:

What is your most common feeling at the end of a working shift or day?

Glad to go home	21%
Frustrated	4%
Satisfied and appreciated	16%
Looking forward to tomorrow	11%
Wish for better things	8%
Proud to have done something worthwhile	40%

Needless to say when the assessment took place in September the staff satisfied the assessor that the hotel met the Standard and they were subsequently recognised as an Investor In People.

Case Study VIII
Toyota Motor Manufacturing (UK) Ltd

The organisation

The company was formed in 1989 as a British company, wholly owned by Toyota Motor Corporation of Japan. It consists of two greenfield sites: at Burnaston, near Derby, which builds cars; and at Deeside, in North Wales, which manufactures engines. Production started in December 1992 and 1,900 people are currently employed. The word used to describe employees in the organisation is 'members'.

From the outset, the company placed a great emphasis on the importance of people, not just with regard to such things as hiring and training but deeper than that, seeking to create the right kind of culture. They began to look at ways of putting into practice some of the key features of TQM, such as:

- putting the customer first;
- demonstrating mutual trust, honesty, openness and respect;
- endeavouring to secure equal treatment for all members, a goal commonly referred to within the organisation as 'single status'.

The company was seeking to produce 'good corporate citizens' who should try to operate in a way that is socially responsible in addition to contributing to the economic and social wellbeing of the community in which they work. All employees should be 'multi-function members', with each having a broad knowledge of different jobs and developing a wide variety of skills additional to those relating solely to the job itself. Such skills are teamwork, and clear and effective communication, up, down and laterally.

Why Investors in People?

Through careful selection and training Toyota (UK) created this environment for their members. So a legitimate question to ask is why did they perceive a need to become involved with the Investors in People process?

The first thing the organisation noted was that the aims and benefits of Investors in People closely matched their own, namely those relating to helping the organisation improve performance through a planned approach to:

- setting and communicating business goals;
- developing people to meet those goals.

This leads to people being able and motivated to do what the organisation needs them to do.

At the same time the company saw that the potential benefits of pursuing Investors in People were in line with what they wanted to achieve, for example:

- improved earnings;
- reduced costs;
- quality;
- motivation;
- customer satisfaction.

What impressed Toyota was that these benefits were not presented as being merely pious hopes but were actually of demonstrable value and had been achieved through the Investors in People process. Having studied all the documentation and having had discussions with their local TEC they concluded that they should already meet the standard. However it was felt that there should be some additional benefits in undertaking and therefore understanding the assessment itself. Recognition would be of value because:

- it would confirm the effectiveness of current arrangements. They had introduced many policies during start-up which required everyone to learn new things and put them into practice. They expected that an external, independent assessment would check that what they thought was happening was happening;
- it would recognise the achievements of their members, 90 per cent of whom had not worked in the car industry before, 98 per cent if you counted only shop-floor members. Everyone had worked hard and they believed Investors in People would show their success;
- it would enhance the reputation of the company. They believed Investors in People status would not be achieved easily and that it could only improve the image of the company in the eyes of their members, customers and suppliers;
- they felt they would gain a number of improvement points for the future. They knew they were not perfect and were always looking for ways continuously to improve their operation;
- interestingly, they also wanted to support a major Government initiative and their local TEC, something very much in line with their philosophy of wanting to be a Good Corporate Citizen.

Having made the decision to pursue Investors in People Toyota started establishing their present position by comparing their existing policies and procedures with the Standard. They concluded they were already close to it. This meant that for them the journey to becoming an Investor in People should not be a difficult or exacting one.

Their first task was to create the portfolio of evidence. The portfolio was then passed to the assessors (there were two of them in this case) who examined the evidence and decided who they would like to interview (the scoping exercise described in Chapter 6). In Toyota they interviewed 70 members, drawn from all categories of employee, over a period of three days. Toyota felt the assessment to be a tough and rigorous process. They would advise that anyone considering undertaking it needs to be absolutely certain they are ready for the assessment.

In Toyota's case the assessors were satisfied that they met the requirements of the Standard and made a recommendation to the local TEC recognition panel who accepted the recommendation and Toyota Motor Manufacturing (UK) Ltd was recognised as an Investor in People in October 1993. Following recognition they received feedback from the assessors which the company are now seeking to put in place as they continue their journey.

They believe that, at the end of the day, the real beneficiaries of their Investors in People techniques are their customers. 98 per cent of their shop-floor members had not built a car before and yet from day one their cars had met the demanding standards set by Toyota Motor Corporation and their customers. This has been confirmed by the achievement of a number of external awards for the British-built Carina E such as being awarded for two years running 'Best Buy' status by the Consumers Association; and 'Most reliable family car' by *What Car?* magazine.

Case Study IX
Uxbridge Magistrates' Court

The organisation

Uxbridge Magistrates' Court is one of the 20 magistrates' courts serving outer London. It serves the London Borough of Hillingdon with a population of 230,000, the third largest of the London Boroughs. The Court is funded by central government (80 per cent) and the local authority (20 per cent). The part of the funding that comes from central government is paid by the Lord Chancellor's Department by means of a grant which is calculated using the following formula:

60 per cent – the number and types of cases completed by the court;

25 per cent – their effectiveness in the enforcement of unpaid fines;

10 per cent – their efficiency in dealing with new cases;

5 per cent – the quality of service provided to Court users.

The court employs 55 staff, 17 on the legal side of the business (including a senior legal manager, lawyer trainees and ushers) and 38 on administration, finance, etc. In line with many public sector organisations, some work, for example court security and catering, has been contracted out to the private sector. In addition the court has 119 Justices of the Peace.

The Magistrates' Courts have not been immune to the move in the public sector to improve cost effectiveness and have been subjected to pressures to reduce financial expenditure. There has been sustained pressure from the Lord Chancellor's Department. These changes were felt to be more significant than any that had taken place during the last 40 years. This led to each of the 20 Magistrates' Courts looking at Investors in People as a means of increasing efficiency through a planned approach to managing change.

The commitment to Investors in People was made in late 1993. The Senior Management Team headed by Martin Hamilton, who had just been appointed, identified very quickly that to offer a quality service and deliver the effectiveness demanded by central government a number of changes needed to be effected:

- the culture of the management team should alter;
- they should plan strategically;
- they should be clear of their direction and purpose and this should be communicated to all staff;
- they needed a business plan and this should include a people dimension, linking training, retraining and human resource planning with clear links to the business strategy.

Needless to say these coincided exactly with the aims of Investors in People.

The journey

This started with a diagnosis against the Standard which came up with results that were at first misleading. It is now felt that staff answered questions in the way that they believed management wanted them to. This led to the consultant who helped with the diagnosis believing very little needed to be done when in fact there was quite a lot to be done. The lesson learnt here was *encourage your staff to be completely honest when answering questions at this stage*. If they are not it will come out later and will delay the process.

Following the completion of the diagnosis an action plan was drawn up but then little happened for a while.

In April, John Millward, the recently appointed Head of Administrative Services was given the task of putting the action plan into practice. This began with the development of a strategic plan on which everything else would be built. One of the priority objectives of the strategic plan was to develop a more professional approach to management. The Senior Management Team agreed that they would move in the direction of competence-based appraisal, which would replace the existing appraisal process, which they felt was not very effective. Judith Nichols, Head of Legal Services, had been responsible in a previous job for a national report on competences for legal staff employed in the Magistrates' Courts Service and was able to use this experience to help all sections of staff at Uxbridge to develop competence frameworks. The new appraisal system was introduced in May 1994. At the same time the strategy was being developed and the first business plan was launched that September.

The first appraisals identified a range of needs that needed to be met. Changes in procedures, such as the withdrawal of the services of the Metropolitan Police as prison escorts, led to the need for a range of training and developmental activities taking place.

The enthusiasm generated by staff throughout this period led to Uxbridge Magistrates' Court coming forward for assessment too early. Although most of the systems were in place the full outcomes had not yet come through. This is always a difficult decision for an assessor, when everything feels right culturally, systems appear to be working but the evidence of evaluation is not quite complete. John Millward felt that they had been victims of their own speed, which is a useful lesson for other organisations – give the systems time to bed in. They also felt that perhaps it was a question of presentation. In spite of this hiccup, they had a number of positive benefits from the Investors in People process:

- the new, competence-based appraisal system is working effectively;
- the new procedures for escorting prisoners are working well;
- everyone is starting to think more strategically. An illustration

of this is the successful introduction of a new rota system for the 119 Justices with the introduction of standby Justices to cover for unexpected absences.

They also feel better equipped to deal with whatever changes emerge in the future.

Uxbridge Magistrates' Court subsequently met the criteria and were recognised as an Investor in People in June 1995.

Case Study X
Vauxhall Motors
(The Luton Manufacturing Plant)

The organisation

Vauxhall Motors is part of General Motors, the world's largest industrial company. The Luton plant assembles Vauxhall Cavaliers and Opel Vectors and currently employs 4,000 people.

Why Investors in People?

Vauxhall have a long-established sophisticated training and development programme. As has often been the case with larger companies, a significant reason for going for Investors in People was external benchmarking.

Personnel Manager, Tony Lines, was the 'champion' for the Investor in People process.

The first decision we had to make was whether to embrace Investors in People as Vauxhall as a whole or on the basis of internal units. As Manufacturing, Luton, we have a significant level of devolved responsibility. Therefore there were some good reasons to apply as a separate unit. The same applies to Ellesmere Port plant and other areas of the company.

It was decided it would be better to achieve the standard locally as that more accurately reflected the management structure and strategy. Responsibilities are devolved to each of the locations of manufacturing. The company has a matrix organisation linking manufacturing plants across Europe.

The separate unit approach was agreed internally. The plant got the go-ahead. Tony Lines said, 'We were keen to get on with it because we'd gone through our Quality Network process, in which devolved responsibility was based on teams, which was a central objective.' The organisation felt that as a result of developing the Quality Network programme they had addressed such issues as access to information, communication, improving the knowledge and skills base of employees and increasing individual responsibility.

> It was clear also to us that if you devolved responsibility then you needed to have the commitment of people to improve their working practices. This commitment to improve is led by knowing what the customer wants and, within people's defined responsibilities, enabling the employee to act as an agent for change.

Investors in People offered the organisation a system compatible with and supportive of what they were currently in the process of doing. 'It takes time. Time to make the changes in the organisation, for people to absorb information, for people to receive training, and time for changing the organisation to accommodate new roles.'

One initial major concern was the amount of paperwork and general bureaucracy the process appeared to demand. With the pressure on and with a range of initiatives already under way, perhaps this was one too many?

> When we examined the process we came to the conclusion that it wasn't as bureaucratic as we initially thought. You can only make these sorts of changes if you do them in a systematic way. You have to know what your objectives are and if you're managed in a proper way then the paperwork is already there. So it's not really about having to create a new batch of paperwork to support the process. It really meant collecting together the things that were already there.

The company operates on the assumption that the customer expects to receive the benefits, in terms of quality of product and service, of a committed and informed workforce. Investors in People offered Vauxhall an opportunity to take on board a process that should ultimately give the customers what they want with one significant advantage: 'It is up to us to determine the process. You can't gain commitment without people being aware of what's going on, without people working together.'

For Vauxhall, therefore, the process enabled them to test out whether their people did actually know what was going on, whether they did know what their responsibilities were, and whether they were properly trained to be able to do their jobs. 'These are the things that produce what the customer wants.'

The company stresses the importance of knowing why training is required in a corporate, departmental and individual context before any measurement of the impact of training can have any reality. 'We want people to understand what their actual job entails and what their contribution is within the framework of their particular activity.'

Vauxhall were interested to recognise the enthusiasm that some employees brought to the delivery of their roles. The measurement of this enthusiasm can be done using certain forms of output. A lot of people are involved in continuous improvement activities and are members of teams. One method employed by the company for measuring this 'enthusiasm' is by looking at the quality and level of output of suggestions for improvement emanating from these groups.

> Everybody has got to be looking at ways in which we can all make improvements. Each team is responsible for examining its own work to see how that could be improved. Sometimes we also put special teams together to work on particular items, taking them out of their normal routine for a while. We regard this as a good example of people development. What we want at Vauxhall is 4,000 people all looking at ways in which we can do our jobs better. Better means a more satisfied and more enthusiastic customer.

Vauxhall is keen to stress that they see the main difference between themselves and their competitors as having committed and informed employees. All have similar access to similar technology. The key, therefore, is how people are developed, supported and empowered. This view integrates well, of course, with the principle tenets of Investors in People. Vauxhall see the key benefits of Investors in People as follows.

- It encourages and can enable a systematic approach to the management of change.
- It allows time for initiatives to be embedded and revisited on a regular basis.
- It offers external benchmarking.
- It facilitates mechanisms supporting and accommodating new roles emerging as a result of change and development.
- It is primarily people focused.
- It promotes empowerment across a wide range of roles and offers the opportunity to promote best practice. 'The people who do the jobs know the most about them.'

Case Study XI
Whitbread Pub Partnerships

The organisation

Whitbread plc is a leading UK food, drinks and leisure company. They own and operate a range of pubs, restaurants, hotels and shops and brew several famous brands of beer. Whitbread employs around 63,000 people and has assets and sales of some £2.5 billion.

John Roberts, the Head of Human Resource Development for Whitbread Pub Partnerships is closely involved with the Investor in People process for the division and contributed the majority of information used in putting this case-study together.

Whitbread corporate objectives are:

- to be the best retailer in drinks and eating out in Britain;
- to grow their own beer business through strong brands and cost effective operations;
- to attract and retain customers by providing better service than their competitors;
- to finance the growth of Whitbread's existing businesses from their own cash flows;
- to acquire new businesses which are financially attractive and a strategic fit;
- to continue to build their distinctive co-operative culture since this improves their competitiveness.

Clearly it is the last objective that significantly contributed to creating the climate for the Investors in People process to be explored.

Whitbread's businesses are managed by four divisions, Whitbread Inns, Whitbread Restaurants and Leisure, the Whitbread Beer Company and Whitbread Pub Partnerships. Whitbread Inns achieved recognition in 1994 and the purpose of this case-study is to feature an organisation that is currently seeking recognition. Of particular interest, though, is the linking by Whitbread Inns of training to the pay structure in a scheme that has become known as 'earning for learning'. In addition, each member of staff participates in a training scheme – Share Inn Success. Staff accrue credit points based on efficiency and performance of pub or regional group. These points can then be exchanged for a variety of goods. Whitbread note in their Briefing Book (1994) that this scheme, coupled with their staff training programme, has helped reduce staff turnover by 30 per cent.

As each business is different, with its own corporate culture, decisions relating to Investors in People were made on a divisional basis. Each area has its own mission statement, focusing on the brand or the business concept they are in. This is the prime driver.

Whitbread Pub Partnerships are currently on the journey towards recognition and it is on this division that this case study focuses.

The organisation

Whitbread Pub Partnerships manages the company's leased pub operations including 2,300 pubs which are mainly on 20-year leases to individual business people. Following a restructuring process this division was formally created in March 1992. Starting from scratch presented a range of opportunities and expectations relating to getting it right first time.

The journey

Investigation and discussion as to the relative merits of pursuing Investors in People began in March 1993. The formal commitment was made in June 1993. Initial estimates suggested that the journey towards recognition should take about two years. However, following further discussions and changes in staffing, the date for assessment has now been set for January 1997.

The process

The division has a flat structure with only four layers, making the skills identification/needs analysis process both more efficient and more accurate. The division is keen not to bring 'the baggage of history' with them, preferring to look ahead at the opportunities downsizing offered in terms of looking further into enhancing people's quality of delivery. This translation from 'old to new' triggered a range of activities including examination, development and agreement of the mission and its meaning, internal attitudinal surveys and working towards a deeper and shared understanding of what the organisation is about and what the individual's place is in it. In effect, in answer to the question 'Why are you going for Investors In People?' the response would be similar to that of Fujitsu – 'we have got a lot in place already; we would welcome the opportunity to benchmark our processes externally.'

Where Whitbread did identify weaknesses, such as those relating to training output, measures were introduced to improve the system. Therefore evaluative procedures are now part of the briefing before training, and during the training itself, the implementation of action points and the review. Stress is placed on ownership of the process by the individual, coupled with the expectation that ownership and empowerment bring with them increased responsibility for the individual to contribute to the management of their own training.

A focus at pub level on business improvement measures has given rise to improved induction procedures for licensees, improved communications, a greater appreciation of the real benefits of training and a reduction of the 'hassle factor' – licensees are more confident because they are better trained and therefore need less day-to-day central direction, thus contributing to greater cost effectiveness.

Research has been undertaken to look at exactly what it is that makes a successful licensee. This was done in part by a questionnaire focusing on what the new licensee needs. A modular training programme based on the analysis of these individual needs was then constructed, giving a menu of training inputs.

There is no corporate unit with responsibility for training. The corporate role for Human Resource Management is that of facilitation in spreading best practice, and strategic planning. The philosophy of the Human Resource team with Whitbread Pub Partnerships is that they are less of a provider and more of an enabler, being a 'group of internal consultants who enable people to do things for themselves'.

With the emphasis on this 'enabling', all managers are for instance required to attend a three-day course designed to improve their training related skills. Operational managers are then responsible for the delivery of a minimum of four group sessions per year. These sessions are planned in consultation with Human Resources who will also help ensure that the training projects are the best available for the identified needs. Ownership and responsibility in training and development, however, lies with the managers themselves.

A common concern echoed by many organisations relates to the involvement and enthusiasm of local line managers with the training process. Giving the line managers this responsibility is an excellent example of embedding training and development throughout the organisation at that critical level (see Chapter 5, The Role of the Line Manager).

A related focus is on the creation of experts within teams. The team culture is very important to the division, and this is supported by the organisational view that off-job answers are not necessarily the right ones. The best learning is learning that takes place on the job.

As has often been asserted throughout this book, written systems are not necessarily the best. (Remember, there is only one piece of required written evidence – see indicator 1.3 in Appendix 1) Take the example of quantification of on-job training. At Whitbread Pub Partnerships the information exists, but not on a database – it is the responsibility of the individual. This, of course, also helps create a climate of trust in which such people-oriented initiatives as Investors in People can flourish and thrive.

Case Study XII
The A Plus Group

The company

The A Plus Group is a marketing and communications company specialising in working for companies primarily in the information technology sector. It currently employs 70 people. This is expected to continue to increase.

It was established in 1981 since when it has consistently achieved over 20% growth per annum. This increased to 35% in 1995. Increased growth was partially brought about by the company gaining a contract with IBM. This contract means that A Plus has the sole responsibility for the development and management of European PR strategy and for the delivery of much of this strategy in the UK. A Plus has developed Euro Plus, a network of affiliates that works throughout Europe, the Middle East and Africa.

In March 1996 Omnicom, the world's largest media group, bought a 20% share in the company. This means that A Plus has preferential access to Omnicom's technology agencies in North America.

A Plus was one of the first 28 companies to be recognised as an Investor in People, in October 1991. It retained this recognition when the company was re-assessed in 1994.

Why Investors in People?

The company had always had a culture of wanting to invest in people so when Investors came along in 1991 it was bound to examine the concept. A Plus found that the framework offered by Investors in People coincided with the company overhauling its HR practices and management structures in preparation for further growth. It offered the ongoing discipline which the company desired if it was to achieve its business targets.

In particular, the company needed to push decision making down the organisation as far as possible requiring people to think and act as defined by best practice. This led to an ongoing skills development and personnel management programme to equip employees to meet these requirements.

The benefits

In 1991 the company was quoted as saying that participation in Investors brought focus to 'a more efficient, planned recruitment and development process, a more structured team approach as well as improved management skills in line with business needs'. So when the third anniversary of Investors in People accreditation approached and re-assessment against the Standard was required the company 'never considered not being re-assessed'.

Prior to re-assessment the company took stock of its processes. Although a great deal of training and development had taken place they had lost the focus on recording and evaluating the development; other priorities had got in the way. The need for re-assessment therefore brought this to their attention and in the time available they were able to put this element of managing the development back at the centre of the agenda and have continued to do so ever since.

Current activity

Since re-assessment the company has gone from strength to strength with the search for quality through continual improvement being a key theme in 1996.

Early in 1995 the Odyssey Project was launched which is a 5 year plan to the year 2000 to increase turnover to £15m. This project involved a structural change taking the directors out of mainstream account handling. It also involved group account directors having a greater responsibility for managing the business day to day and managing the development of people. In order to develop existing skills even further to meet these new and extended business goals the company developed a 3 year strategic training plan.

Part of this strategy involved the development of what it considers to be the most advanced training programme in the PR industry. The Professional Excellence Programme (PEP) is a modular programme in six stages linking into different levels within the organisation. It was developed to A Plus' specification with external contractors. It is competency based with exercises assessed by line managers and a newly appointed part time training director. By spring 1996 the programme had already been re-assessed and refined to include a revised induction programme for new starters and a programme focusing specifically on developments in technology. As well as all account staff going through the PEP programme the company is starting to build a competency-based PEP programme for administrative staff.

As part of fulfilling its mission to be the 'first choice consultance for global IT companies', A Plus has developed a Staff Exchange Programme (STEP) through Euro Plus which involves A Plus staff working with their affiliates in continental Europe and Scandinavia. The company intend to extend this programme to the US through STEP-UP.

The need for continuous improvement

The company considers itself to be at the 'fast end of the fastest moving sector'. A Plus needs to look constantly for improvements through formal and informal client feedback, benchmarking and learning through the job. A Customer Service Charter is being developed as part of a quality programme.

The company is revising job descriptions, appraisal forms and the processes by which training is evaluated. It is also developing a more sophisticated method of analysing training needs as part of the Personnel Manager's IPD development programme.

With all this activity taking place A Plus is confident that when re-assessment comes around again in 1997 it will be well placed to retain its status as an Investor in People.

In this final section we seek to do three things:

- look beyond initial recognition;
- locate the process in a broader organisational development context;
- make a few suggestions as to sources of help for organisations at any stage of the process.

CHAPTER 10

Maintaining and Retaining Recognition

This chapter will be of potential interest and value to most readers as it covers what happens once recognition has been achieved. The type, style and nature of feedback given to the organisation by the assessor is described, as well as how the TEC will seek to maintain contact during the period between recognition and the date when reassessment is due. It also examines some of the issues currently being debated about the reassessment process following the experience of the first organisations to undergo this process.

Why three years?

Recognition as an Investor in People lasts for three years. Organisations of all shapes and sizes ask the question – why wait as long as three years? Originally the idea was that recognition could last for a maximum of three years and it would be up to TECs to decide if they wanted to reassess within that period. Most TECs indicated they were likely to wait the full three year period before reassessing. To maintain national consistency it was decided that there would be no optional time-frame and all recognitions should last for three years. Consideration of a number of factors gave rise to the view that three years is an appropriate period of time. These can be summarised as follows:

- Investors in People concerns strategic planning. It is possible that some organisations may not be able to demonstrate some of the significant improvements and benefits in less than that period;
- There was a commonly held view felt that organisations would understandably question the logic of having an assessment every year in terms of cost and added value;
- TECs would not be able to cope with the resource implications of reassessing every year.

The first reassessments

Following the very first recognitions in 1991, TECs were encouraged to maintain contact with recognised organisations. This contact could be on an informal basis but a dialogue was encouraged that would indicate to the TEC whether the organisation was continuing to demonstrate its commitment to being an Investor in People.

In practice, contact was maintained initially because the first organisations to be recognised were frequently invited to speak at events hosted by TECs and other interested organisations. However, evidence from the first reassessments indicates that the contact during the three year period was not always as structured as had been planned and expected. Many organisations therefore were left unsupported and uninformed as to what the reassesment process would involve. It is inappropriate to apportion blame for this situation, although the government at the time had set targets to be achieved over a period shorter than most informed sources thought appropriate. Attention was focused on increasing the number of organisations that were making the commitment to become Investors in People and on carrying out assessments of those that had completed the 'journey'.

Three years seemed a long way away and the issue of reassessment was, in the main, set aside to be dealt with in due course. In addition, the turnover of TEC staff at this time was particularly high. This was especially true in the case of those staff who were seconded civil servants wishing to return to the service. This compounded the difficulty as they were replaced by staff who needed to learn a great deal very quickly.

Most of the organisations first assessed were given little, if any, feedback and therefore did not have an agreed agenda for the three year period. Although attempts were made over the ensuing three year period to offer guidance and support with regard to reassessment, it was evident that what was needed for the future was regular, structured contact *throughout* the three year period.

As with any new process the skills and expertise of the people involved developed and, although the process that the first organisations experienced is more or less the same as the current process, the manner in which it is carried out has been refined considerably into a far more sophisticated and rigorous process. In other words, lessons have been learned, assessors are now much more skilled and the whole quality assurance process is much enhanced.

Post assessment feedback to organisation

The first significant lesson learnt from the early assessments underpinned the importance of offering feedback to organisations, following the decision by the recognition panel to recognise an organisation.

One of the benefits of an external assessor examining the processes and systems within an organisation is that they invariably discover that although processes and systems are working effectively, they can always be improved. This has been further encouraged by recognition panels who are increasingly very suspicious of assessors' reports of organisations that appear 'too good'. Assessors are therefore encouraged to present a picture which is realistic and includes issues that, although meeting the requirements of the standard, could be improved. Recognition panels themselves also offer assessors a range of items that they would like fed back to organisations.

Frequently the feedback concerns issues about evaluation. Although organisations may have demonstrated sufficient evidence to meet the requirements of the indicators, it is often clear to assessors that there are opportunities to have objectives, targets and standards that are better focused which will lead to improved evaluation.

Normally the feedback is given by the assessor with an advisor from the TEC present. The assessor will then withdraw and the advisor will discuss with the representative of the organisation how these issues can be taken forward and whether the TEC can offer support.

In the spirit of *kaizen* (the search for a better way), most organisations welcome this feedback. The feedback, in effect, sets part of the agenda for the next three years and in reality starts the reassessment process. Some TECs have encouraged organisations to develop an action plan for the three year period. There is a debate as to exactly how detailed this plan should be, covering as it does such a long period.

Many TECs have encouraged organisations who have been recognised to continue networking to support one another throughout the three years.

The evolution of the portfolio

The majority of the first batch of portfolios were very different in style content and presentation to those being presented to assessors today. This was a second major lesson learned. Portfolios have become, in the main, much more streamlined and better presented.

Initially it was felt the portfolio would be a universally useful document, particularly for smaller organisations. The expectation was that the portfolio, the production of which may have been the first time an organisation had collated material, would evolve into their Training and Development Manual. Some organisations were therefore encouraged to maintain and update it as a useful exercise. For other organisations it was agreed that it might not be a useful task. It was left, therefore, to each organisation to decide what was best for them. It was recommended that the portfolio was kept intact as it might be useful for the assessor at the reassessment stage.

It appears from the first reassessments that most organisations developed a second portfolio and the first one was of marginal use.

Lessons learned from the first reassessments

Lessons are still being learned as the process is relatively new. However, as mentioned earlier, because of the increased skills of the assessors, the process of reassessment for most organisations might well have been experienced differently. For example, the first assessments placed more emphasis on the portfolio of evidence than on site visit and interviews. This does not happen today. Far more emphasis is now placed on individual responses to the assessor and this is now regarded as the 'acid test' as to whether an organisation is actually an Investor in People.

TECs probably have not maintained sufficient structured contact, especially with the early recognised organisations, during the three year period.

The excitement and enthusiasm generated by undertaking the journey and achieving recognition typically soon passes and things begin to plateau. Systems atrophy, if care is not taken to review and modify them to keep them fresh and motivate people (especially line managers) to continue to use them. It is at this point that the additional indicator (4.5) may help. The indicator states that: 'Action takes place to implement improvements to training and development identified as a result of evaluation.'

As mentioned in Chapter 8, in order to satisfy an assessor that this indicator is met, organisations will be expected as part of their evaluation to evaluate continuously the effectiveness of the training and development processes. If this happens, systems that are not being used effectively should be identified and either replaced or developed.

Some organisations may feel, as noted by Tony Miller of Frizzell Financial Services in one of the case-studies, that reassessment has offered little added value. While this needs to change it is clear that not all organisations feel this way. The A Plus case-study illustrates that the need to take stock prior to the reassessment process alerted them to the fact that, because of other priorities, they had lost the focus on recording and evaluating the development that had taken place. Clearly the discipline of being reassessed ensures that organisations will not let systems atrophy.

The continuing development and refinement of the reassessment process

In 1993 the Board of Investors in People UK laid down the following principle, the overriding message being that once the organisation had proved that they had met the Standard, the purpose of the reassessment was to prove that they had maintained it. This meant that:

- the credibility of the Standard should be maintained;
- there is a need to avoid unnecessary bureaucracy and cost;
- the reassessment should be business-plan driven;
- it should focus on changes; and
- it should be completed within the third anniversary of the original assessment.

The Board stated that the process should comprise:

- an examination of the accumulated evidence, original portfolio and the assessor report;
- interviews with a small sample of employees to confirm that the original and any new arrangements are in place and working effectively;
- a report by the assessor to a recognition panel;
- a decision by the panel.

After the first reassessments, because there was some dissatisfaction with the process, there was a debate about what the reassessment process should be. A project was commissioned in 1995 to examine the issues around reassessment. From this project a model has emerged. However at the time of writing the debate is continuing.

The results of the project showed that a key concern among employers was, although there were some exceptions, the lack of TEC/LEC contact between assessments. Also, in most cases there was no funding to help organisations prepare for reassessment.

Because all the organisations that were involved in the project had undergone major changes during the three year period, a major reassessment was invariably needed, and the majority questioned the benefit when faced with the costs of such a reassessment. Larger organisations were looking to develop an integrated management approach to quality and therefore were in favour of internalising the assessment process with some form of external verification.

The emerging model

The project model involves organisations, once they have been recognised, drawing up an agreement with the Assessment Unit which will involve a 'service agreement' for maintenance of the Standard. This would offer a number of services to the organisation which may include:

- a series of annual monitoring visits, by an assessor, and agreed development actions against the Standard on an ongoing basis with a smaller and lower cost three-year review.
- where appropriate, organisations could be encouraged to train (on an approved course) and develop internal 'monitors' who would facilitate an internal review of progress and achievement against the Investors in People Standard and any other related quality standards.

There is also an option, for those who want it, of the status quo; in other words a portfolio of evidence followed by site visits.

At the time of writing, these proposals were being refined, following consultation with TECs/LECs, after which they will be piloted with a number of assessment units.

The future

Assessor relationships

Although initially there was a debate about whether the original assessor should be used for reassessments, in practice most reassessments have been undertaken by a different assessor, although the guidelines do not insist that this is the case. However, the above maintenance model may open up this debate again. To make such an arrangement work effectively it may be necessary to use the same assessor but then, with regular contact, will the assessor become less objective?

Feedback at the end of the assessment

This continues to be debated by assessors. Clearly assessors need to continue to develop their ability to offer constructive feedback following assessments. The added value of external assessment, and reassessment, will mainly be derived from this feedback.

Other issues

Although a number of these issues have been mentioned throughout this book we thought it may be useful to highlight those that are either currently being debated or piloted by the various stakeholders associated with Investors in People such as Investors in People UK, TECs, LECs and so on. They include:

- Quality Assurance of the stages that precede assessment, in particular the role of the consultant/adviser. A document produced by Investors in People UK called *The Practitioner Role Guide* sets out minimum standards that should be expected for those people working in key roles associated with the delivery of Investors in People. Among those roles is the role of the adviser. In addition work is progressing on the development of adviser quality assurance arrangements, which involve a competency-based approach. These arrangements are being piloted in a number of areas.
- TEC budgets are clearly under pressure and there is a need to

be innovative about how support to employers can be maintained in such a climate.

- There will be an ongoing debate about the future role of recognition panels.
- Further work to raise the status of the Standard internationally will continue. As part of this process a pilot has been developed involving Investors in People UK working with eight multi-national organisations over a period of 18–24 months.
- At the time of writing, some 18 Australian organisations are approaching assessment.
- Discussions are also taking place with a view to piloting in Denmark, Germany and USA.
- Links will be explored with other quality awards, most notably the European Quality Award which is administered by the European Foundation for Quality Management (EFQM).

CHAPTER 11

Learning to be a Learning Organisation

As we have illustrated throughout this book, the Investors in People process offers support in improving and developing the individual, the unit and the organisation in line with business objectives. As a vehicle promoting and supporting the management of change and an instrument designed to encourage empowerment of employees, Investors in People is potentially a very powerful process. The experience of organisations in our case-studies confirms this.

This chapter looks at how Investors in People can support this process of managing and achieving systemic organisation-wide change by setting it in the wider context of what it means to be a learning organisation. It will be of particular interest to trainers and developers, students, and managers with an interest in a corporate approach to enhancing individuals' contribution to continuous improvement.

What is a learning organisation?

The concept of a 'learning organisation' developed, as we noted earlier, out of the self-development movement from the 1970s onwards, which clearly stressed each individual person's responsibility for addressing his/her own training and career development needs. In many cases people experienced this very positively but all too often inflexible organisational structures, entrenched centralist policies or lack of recognition by the organisation itself of such self-development actions on the part of individual employees, acted as real barriers to self-development in practice.

Gradually it was suggested that it was organisations that needed to be open to, and value, learning for themselves as total entities: learning for organisations as well as learning for individuals in organisations. This idea was encapsulated in 'the learning organisation' literature from the late 1980s and is clearly of increasing use and value for the 1990s as Investors in People continues to attract more and more organisations. There are a number of views as to what exactly a learning organisation is. Some of these are summarised below for the interested reader, otherwise skip to the section that summarises the main characteristics.

Definitions

John Burgoyne has offered the following working definition of a learning organisation: 'A learning organisation continuously transforms itself in the process reciprocally linked to the development of all its members.'

Alternatively Mills and Friesen have described it as follows: 'We conceive of a learning organisation as one able to sustain consistent innovation or "learning", with the immediate goals of improving quality, enhancing customer or supplier relationships, more effectively executing business strategy, and the ultimate objective of sustaining profitability.'

What are the main characteristics of a learning organisation?

Based on research from a number of organisations, some 11 characteristics of a learning organisation have been identified. These characteristics describe a learning organisation in practical terms and are listed below.

1. *A learning approach to strategy or policy*, whereby the very way an organisation decides collectively what to do and how to implement it, with ongoing monitoring and review, and adaptation of plans along the way, is itself a learning process.
2. *Participative policy-making*, which involves as many people as possible in the policy-making process, resulting in better local implementation and greater commitment and ownership of the plan(s), or as Burgoyne states, 'This may take much longer than it might when policy is decided by a small private group of people but what you lose in the extra discussion and thinking time you get back in the implementation time.'
3. *Informing*, using open information systems to make key information available as widely as possible throughout the organisation, which supports participative policy-making (above) but also provides the foundation for all the other characteristics.
4. *Formative accounting and control*, the provision of up-to-date information about the potential consequences of various actions in order to assist in local decision-making and in making changes in a more timely way.
5. *Mutual adjustment between departments*, the importance of each department or part of an organisation viewing itself as a customer of, or supplier to, another department or unit (emanating from a TQM philosophy) and pro-actively working alongside one another rather than only to top–down control.
6. *Reward flexibility*, having available within organisations the right kind of rewards and conditions for individuals in ways which reinforce learning.
7. *Adaptable structures*, possessing the ability to change structures and procedures relatively easily and cheaply.

8. *Boundary workers as environmental scanners*, the ability of organisations to learn about their environments from their own people, particularly those who interact directly with the customer at the internal (departmental) and external (client interface) boundaries.

9. *Inter-organisational learning*, the encouragement of everyone in the whole organisation to learn from everyone else, including internal and external suppliers.

10. *A particular kind of culture and climate*, a climate that promotes learning, including positive learning from mistakes ('it's all right to make a mistake once but it is not all right to make the same mistake two or three times') and a leadership style that encourages taking some responsible risks but offers support and two-way communication throughout.

11. *Self-development opportunities for all*, whereby people have some degree of self-management and self-control over their own development and career progression, but that this self-development philosophy is guided, facilitated and resourced by the organisation. How some of these characteristics of learning for organisations and the principles underlying the Investors in People initiative were realised in practice have been described in our case-studies.

Benchmarking the learning organisation

It is our contention that subscribing to the Investors in People process demands the creation of a learning organisation. In Part Two, the organisations featured in our case-studies demonstrated in practice the value of investing in people. They all exhibit many of the characteristics of a learning organisation. Most have:

- a culture that values and rewards learning ;
- personal and professional development integrated into strategic planning;
- systems and specialists that are used to enhance personal and professional development;

- clear development and support offered equally to all staff throughout their time with the organisation and at all stages of their career;
- a clear and well articulated link between development and appraisal;
- evaluation as an integral part of the personal and professional development iterative loop.

The potential of Investors in People is rooted, as we have noted, in its training and development orientation. Most organisations are engaged in the provision of the training and professional development of existing and future employees, and many may well have acquired already either a TQM award or a quality assurance standard such as ISO 9000/BS5750. It might well be perceived as advantageous by their present and potential customers to pursue Investors in People.

The other significant tenet of Investors in People is its direct link with 'business' objectives. It has to be hoped that the development of clear objectives for the organisation and its constituent units, and explaining these objectives to all staff, will engender that essential sense of ownership via an understanding of what needs to be achieved and what every individual's contribution is.

Conclusion

The Investors in People Standard cannot be achieved without clear evidence of commitment at the highest level; the managing director/ chief executive will be formally interviewed by the assessor and the response will be set against other (formal and informal) interviews/ conversations that the assessor will have over the final formal assessment period. Recognition will not be gained unless a clear corporate approach is reflected by a critical proportion of the staff.

The central theme of this chapter is, therefore, that the Investors in People process is not only about training but also about practically adding value to an organisation's existing and future assets. It is more than a mere paper exercise and it is not a bureaucratic strait-jacket. On the contrary, it offers a positive process in support of change management that is essentially qualitative.

CHAPTER 12

Sources of Help

This Chapter is a 'who's who' of the various sources of help available to assist organisations through the process. As addresses and telephone numbers can soon become out of date it does not give full details of all the sources. It does not attempt to list all sources but merely points to the key players who in turn may have their own sources to which they redirect anyone who wants to know more.

1 Investors in People UK

Investors in People UK was established in July 1993 as a private company limited by guarantee. It opened for business on 1 October 1993. Originally based in Sheffield it moved to premises at 7/10 Chandos Street, London W1M 9DE in April 1994. The role of Investors in People UK is:

- to guard, lead and direct the Investors in People National Standard;
- to define the assessment process in outline;
- national promotion and support;

- national quality assurance;
- assessment and recognition of national organisations, TECs/
  LECs and Industry Training Organisations.

Investors in People UK works in close consultation with all its
partners.

2   Training and Enterprise Councils (TECs)

Training and Enterprise Councils were set up by the government
in the late 1980s to deliver products and services such as youth and
adult training, establish education partnerships and generally
support Enterprise start-up in specific geographical areas
throughout England and Wales.

TECs are independent companies limited by guarantee and driven
strategically by a Board of Directors drawn in the main from key
people in local business communities but also from the public and
voluntary sector. The Board's role is to ensure that the portfolio of
services offered meets the local needs. There are now 81 TECs in
the UK, working in partnership with other key local organisations
that are key players in the economic regeneration of their areas.

They also have the task of encouraging employers to train and
develop their existing workforce in order to develop the skillbase
on which the future prosperity of the country will be based, which
is where Investors in People fits in. TECs are responsible for the
local delivery of Investors in People. This means they are responsible
for marketing and promotion, advice and guidance, assessment and
recognition. TECs deliver this in a variety of ways. All receive
funding from central government, mainly from the Department for
Education and Employment, to help support enterprise activities.
This budget has gradually been reduced and therefore financial
support for Investors in People from TECs is limited and varies from
one TEC to another.

The number of staff working on Investors in People also varies
from TEC to TEC, with most using outside help to deliver the
initiative. Later in this chapter the role of this outside help, mainly
in the form of consultants, is described.

An increasing number of TECs are offering workshops or seminars that are geared to helping organisations through the process. Some TECs will offer these free and others will make a nominal charge. If nothing else, these workshops will introduce you to other organisations that are going through the process and will often be very willing to share ideas, problems, etc.

One of the authors has been closely associated with West London TEC and an example of the workshops on offer there are:

- the line manager's role in Investors in People;
- the internal adviser;
- setting objectives, targets and standards for evaluation;
- building your portfolio.

Other TECs will offer similar workshops.

3   The Universities' and Colleges' Staff Development Agency (UCoSDA)

The Universities' and Colleges' Staff Development Agency (UCoSDA) was created in 1989. It is one of the agencies of the Committee of Vice Chancellors and Principals

UCoSDA seeks to provide advice, support and resources to its member universities and colleges in the planning, organisation, provision and evaluation of continuing professional/vocational development for all personnel in the higher education sector.

It currently employs two approved Investors in People Assessors – including one of the authors of this book. The UCoSDA philosophy captures some of the central themes of this book and is summarised as follows :

Investment in the personal, professional and vocational development of all staff employed by universities and colleges is fundamental

(a)   to the successful achievement of organisational goals and

(b)   to the motivation and continuing capacity of individual staff members to support that achievement.

UCoSDA has produced a number of briefing papers and other publications on Investors in People and related issues and can be contacted at the following address:

Ingram House
65 Wilkinson Street
The University of Sheffield
Sheffield
S10 2GJ
Tel: 0114 282 4211
Fax: 0114 272 8705

4   Scotland – Local Enterprise Companies (LECs)

The position in Scotland is different. LECs were set up at about the same time as TECs but they have a wider remit as they not only took over the delivery of products and services such as Youth and Adult Training but also embraced the role of the Scottish Development Agency and the Highlands and Islands Development Agency.

LECs are private companies limited by guarantee who are contracted to either Scottish Enterprise or Highlands and Islands Enterprise. There are 22 LECs although some counts might show 23, as one straddles the border between Scottish Enterprise and Highlands and Islands Enterprise and is often counted twice.

Assessment and recognition is carried out by Investors in People Scotland so the role of the LECs is to carry out the same work as TECs minus assessment and recognition. They too use outsiders to deliver various stages of Investors in People.

The telephone numbers and addresses of LECs can be found in local telephone directories.

5   Northern Ireland: Training and Employment Agency (T&EA)

The Training and Employment Agency was established as an agency of the Northern Ireland Civil Service in 1990. It carries out a role similar to that of the Employment Department and Employment Agency in Britain (ie a training and job broking service).

One of its divisions has a particular remit to support business and it is under this requirement that Investors in People sits.

The Agency has broadly the same role as the TECs in delivering Investors in People. However, the financial support offered by the Agency is through the Agency's Company Development Programme and the consultants who deliver it.

6   Investors in People Scotland

The role of Investors in People Scotland has been described in Chapter 7, The Recognition Process.

7   Management Charter Initiative (MCI)

For information on the Management Standards or the report *Investors in People and the Management Standards* contact MCI at the following address:

Russell Square House
10–12 Russell Square
London WC1B 5BZ
Tel: 0171 972 9000

8   Industry Training Organisations (ITOs)

ITOs act as the principal focal point for training matters in their particular sector of industry. Their tasks are to see that the skills needs of their sector are being met and that appropriate standards are established and maintained for key occupations in their sector. There are about 120 ITOs – one for most industrial sectors of the country.

Nearly all ITOs are employer led and funded bodies set up by employers for employers and are often linked to existing employer associations.

A number of ITOs may be able to offer support through the Investors in People process. There is a National Council of ITOs (NCITO) that can supply more information. Their address is:

5 George Lane
Royston
Herts
SG8 9AR
Tel: 01763 247285

9   Consultants and consultancy organisations

Feelings about using consultants differ considerably from one organisation (or person) to another. This section does not intend to debate the relative merits of using consultants. The arguments are well rehearsed elsewhere. However, because the resources within TECs and LECs are limited, most, if not all, use outside help to deliver the various stages of Investors in People.

Because they are so reliant on using consultants most TECs and LECs have adopted a variety of criteria for establishing the ability of the consultants to deliver what is required. This varies from quality assurance through outside bodies to drawing up internal criteria to establish a preferred list of consultants.

Investors in People UK are also taking an interest in this subject as the credibility of the process of becoming an Investor in People can be affected considerably if the advice and guidance given has not been good. There are a number of examples of assessments being deferred because of bad or misleading advice.

Choosing and using consultants

So what can be done? The first stage is to be clear what it is you want the consultant to do. This may involve a discussion with someone from the Investors team at the local TEC or LEC.

The next stage is to ensure that the consultant is qualified to deliver what you want. This is probably easier said than done as there are so many consultants touting for work. Some simple questions may be to ask:

- How many companies have they helped to achieve recognition?
- Which TECs/LECs are they working with?
- What training have they had in connection with Investors in People?
- Are they an approved assessor? How many assessments have they carried out?
- What is their approach to helping organisations achieve Investors in People status? (Beware those consultants who will get it for you and have a sure fire way of meeting a number of indicators! They may sell you a package that you don't want or need.)
- What sector expertise do they bring? In some cases having a sector expertise may save time with interpreting the Standard but it is not always essential.

How consultants can help

Provided you get the right consultant they can help in a number of ways. First they may have experience working with TECs and may help you secure some financial support. They should have experience of carrying out certain tasks and can therefore help you avoid reinventing wheels.

They *should* know what is expected of you by an assessor but ensure that you are not merely introducing things for an assessor but are doing them for sound business reasons too. In most cases the needs of the assessor will coincide with your needs but you need to challenge the consultant constantly, or TEC staff for that matter, if you feel you are being asked to do something from which you will feel no business benefits.

When consultants can help

1. diagnosis and action planning;
2. advice and guidance with implementation of plans;
3. assessment.

Diagnosis and action planning

To get an honest response from staff it is often necessary to use an outsider to help carry out this stage of the process. It is also the stage when you will be least able to interpret the responses against the indicators, so bringing in a consultant experienced in carrying out this exercise will save a lot of time.

The main health warning here concerns the writing of the action plan. Consultants should carry out the diagnosis and analysis against the indicators and present the issues to you. These issues should cover those indicators that appear to be satisfied and those not. Generally they can be grouped under a number of headings (see Chapter 8). It is the job of the people within the organisation to decide how they want to tackle these issues. A good consultant will stand back at this stage and allow you to do this. They may help you present the action plan, filling in stages that may have been overlooked or presenting it in a way that meets TEC requirements if funding is being sought. We have seen too many action plans written by consultants that have not been implemented because they are not owned by the organisation for whom they were written.

Advice and guidance with implementation of plans

The action plan should include what external help you may need to help you through the process. We believe this should be kept to a minimum as most organisations, even small ones, should be able to devise and introduce most of the systems, processes and practices which they need to meet their business requirements and at the same time meet the requirements of the indicators. There are of course a number of exceptions, such as introducing strategic planning for the first time, or introducing an appraisal process, but remember this is *not* a requirement of the Standard. Most organisations will need some kind of management development, even if it's only looking at the requirements of the indicators, and it is helpful to have an outsider facilitate this.

Be careful about consultants who try to persuade you that you need large amounts of consultancy input to meet the Standard, though experience has shown that most organisations will need some 'handholding' through the process. This will involve attendance at meetings to discuss progress and nudge the organisation along.

When it comes to building a portfolio, outside help from someone who understands how to present your case to an assessor will be useful. Some TECs/LECs will offer this service but with others you may need a consultant.

Assessment

This is one stage where you may have no option about having a consultant in your organisation. The TEC, or other Assessment and Recognition Unit, decides who will carry out the assessment and their policy may be to use consultants for this role. Any dissatisfaction with the assessor should be reported back to the TEC Investors Manager or Assessment Unit Manager.

Other organisations

The help offered by peers who are going through the process was mentioned earlier but what about those organisations who have already been recognised? The first organisations were inundated by callers who wanted to know how they did it; some of them may well have wondered why they got involved. However now there are a lot more people to offer this kind of guidance.

Most TECs and LECs invite representatives from recognised organisations to speak at local events so you may well find out about them then. If not, or if you need to identify a specific type of organisation, your TEC or LEC will be able to help identify and put you in touch with someone who can help.

Investors in People material, videos, etc

Finally, there is a wealth of material available to help you work through the process. Most TECs have produced their own material but in addition there is a lot of nationally available material produced by Investors in People UK. There is also a lot of material in the form of articles in management and training magazines and books (this is one!) either being developed or already in existence to help develop an understanding of what Investors in People is and how it can promote organisational development.

Appendix 1
The National Standard for Effective Investment in People

Principle One: Commitment

An Investor in People makes a commitment from the top to develop all employees to achieve its business objectives.

1.1 The commitment from top management to train and develop employees is communicated effectively throughout the organisation.
1.2 Employees at all levels are aware of the broad aims or vision of the organisation.
1.3 The employer has considered what employees at all levels will contribute to the success of the organisation, and has communicated this effectively to them.
1.4 Where representative structures exist, communication takes place between management and representatives on the vision of where the organisation is going and the contribution that employees (and their representatives) will make to its success.

Principle Two: Planning

An Investor in People regularly reviews the needs and plans the training and development of all employees.

2.1 A written but flexible plan sets out the organisation's goals and targets.
2.2 A written plan identifies the organisation's training and development needs, and specifies what action will be taken to meet these needs.

2.3   Training and development needs are regularly reviewed against goals and targets at the organisation, team and individual level.

2.4   A written plan identifies the resources that will be used to meet training and development needs.

2.5   Responsibility for training and developing employees is clearly identified and understood throughout the organisation, starting at the top.

2.6   Objectives are set for training and development actions at the organisation, team and individual level.

2.7   Where appropriate, training and development needs are linked to external standards such as National Vocational Qualifications (NVQs) or Scottish Vocational Qualifications (SVQs) and units.

Principle Three: Action

An Investor in People takes action to train and develop individuals on recruitment and throughout their employment.

3.1   All new employees are introduced effectively to the organisation and all employees new to a job are given the training and development they need to do that job.

3.2   Managers are effective in carrying out their responsibilities for training and developing employees.

3.3   Managers are actively involved in supporting employees to meet their training and development needs.

3.4   All employees are made aware of the training and development opportunities open to them.

3.5   All employees are encouraged to help identify and meet their job-related training and development needs.

3.6   Action takes place to meet the training and development needs of individuals, teams and the organisation.

Principle Four: Evaluation

An Investor in People evaluates the investment in training and development to assess achievement and improve future effectiveness.

4.1   The organisation evaluates the impact of training and development actions on knowledge, skills and attitude.

4.2   The organisation evaluates the impact of training and development actions on performance.

4.3   The organisation evaluates the contribution of training and development to the achievement of its goals and targets.

4.4   Top management understands the broad costs and benefits of training and developing employees.

4.5   Action takes place to implement improvements to training and development identified as a result of evaluation.

4.6   Top management's continuing commitment to training and developing employees is demonstrated to all employees.

Appendix 2
Investors in People: Manager's Survey

Please tick the most relevant of the boxes on the right.

	Yes	No	Unsure
1. Is the organisation committed to training and developing its people?	☐	☐	☐
2. Does the organisation have a clear vision of how it will develop?	☐	☐	☐
3. If yes, has it been communicated to all staff?	☐	☐	☐
4. Does the organisation have a written business plan?	☐	☐	☐
5. If yes, does it identify broad training and development needs?	☐	☐	☐
6. Are all staff clear how their role contributes to helping the organisation meet its business plan?	☐	☐	☐
7. Do you believe that you are competent to manage your staff and their development?	☐	☐	☐
8. Are the training and development needs of all staff reviewed on a regular basis?	☐	☐	☐
9. Does this review lead to a training and development plan for all staff?	☐	☐	☐
10. Do you actively encourage and support all your staff in developing their skills?	☐	☐	☐
11. Is there an induction programme for all new staff?	☐	☐	☐
12. Following training and/or development activities do you ensure that staff are using any newly acquired skills?	☐	☐	☐
13. Do you believe training and development helps the organisation achieve its business goals?	☐	☐	☐
14. Do you assess the costs and benefits of training and development activities?	☐	☐	☐

Appendix 3
Investors in People: Employee's Survey

Please read each question carefully, then tick one of the boxes on the right. If you feel the question does not apply or that you do not know the answer you should tick the third box.

	Yes	No	Unsure
1. Has the top management told you about their commitment to developing the skills and knowledge of everyone in the organisation?	☐	☐	☐
2. Could you explain to someone who does not work for the organisation what it is trying to achieve?	☐	☐	☐
3. Do you understand how your job contributes to the success of the organisation?	☐	☐	☐
4. Do you know who is responsible for helping you acquire the skills and knowledge that you need to do your job?	☐	☐	☐

When you first joined the organisation:

	Yes	No	Unsure
5. Were you given information about how the organisation works?	☐	☐	☐
6. Did you take part in a training programme?	☐	☐	☐
7. If you have changed jobs within the organisation, did you get any support to enable you to understand your new role?	☐	☐	☐
8. Do you and your manager regularly review your training and development needs?	☐	☐	☐

9. Within the last twelve months have you received any support to help you do your job?   ☐ ☐ ☐

10. Have you been encouraged to work towards a qualification relevant to your job?   ☐ ☐ ☐

11. Do you know how to find out about learning opportunities that may be open to you?   ☐ ☐ ☐

12. Does your line manager encourage you to identify any new skills you need to do your job?   ☐ ☐ ☐

13. When it has been agreed that action is required, does it happen?   ☐ ☐ ☐

14. Does your manager help you develop the skills you need to do your job?   ☐ ☐ ☐

15. Are you told about opportunities to learn new skills and update your knowledge?   ☐ ☐ ☐

16. Before participating in any learning activity do you agree with your manager what you are expected to learn?   ☐ ☐ ☐

17. After you have worked through a learning activity does your manager,

    (a) discuss whether your skills have improved?   ☐ ☐ ☐

    (b) check whether you are putting your new skills into practice?   ☐ ☐ ☐

18. Overall do you feel that the organisation offers you the opportunity to learn new skills and develop yourself?   ☐ ☐ ☐

Appendix 4
Sample Size Guidelines

Number of staff employed	Sample band
0–5	100%
6–15	100–60%
16–25	70–40%
26–50	60–30%
51–75	50–25%
76–100	40–20%
101–125	30–15%
126–500	20–10%
501–1,000	15–5%
1,001–2,500	8–4%
2,501–5,000	4–2%
5,000+	3–1%

Assessors should use their judgement when using the guidance above and bear in mind that, for example, where the number of staff is 76 it does not automatically require a sample of 40%. It may require 20% – depending on circumstances.

Source: Investors in People UK

Index